Jacket Jazz

Five Great Looks . . . Over 30 Patchwork Techniques

by Judy Murrah

CREDITS

Editor . . . . Barbara Weiland
Copy Editor . . . . Liz McGehee
Text and Cover Design . . . . Joanne Lauterjung
Formatting . . . . ArtWorks
Photography . . . . Brent Kane
Illustration and Graphics . . . . Laurie Osborne-Clay
                                                                    Laurel Strand
                                                                    Stephanie Benson
Pattern Grading . . . . Jane Whiteley

Special thanks to Tom Hobbs and Carl Badgett of Hallmark Pianos in Woodinville, Washington, for the use of their store for photography, and to Marion Shelton for the use of her home.

Jacket Jazz ©
© 1993 by Judy Murrah

That Patchwork Place, Inc., PO Box 118, Bothell, WA 98041-0118 USA

Published in the United States of America
Printed in the British Crown Colony of Hong Kong
98 97 96 95 94 93   6 5 4 3 2

Library of Congress Cataloging-in-Publication Data
Murrah, Judy
        Jacket jazz / Judy Murrah.
                p.   cm.
        ISBN 1-56477-021-4 :
        1. Coats. 2. Patchwork–Patterns. 3. Quilted goods. I. Title.
TT535M87   1993
746.9'2–dc20
                                                                    93-7120
                                                                    CIP

✓ Dedication

To the two people who have had the greatest influence on my personal and business life: Tommy Murrah, my helpmate and the love of my life since age 14, and Karey Bresenhan, my mentor and the best and truest friend I've ever had.

✓ Acknowledgments

My deep appreciation goes to:

My mom, Ruby Earl Olafson, who encouraged me and allowed me, as a six-year-old, to use her Singer sewing machine;

My children, Todd, Holly, and Troy, who wore my first efforts at "Wearable Art";

The shopkeepers, Rebbecca Matusek, Bev Harding, Barbara and Ron Goldkorn, and Billie Stehling, who have consistently given me an audience for teaching my jacket designs;

All my students (sometimes lovingly called "groupies"), who eagerly anticipate each new jacket design;

Jewel Patterson, from whom I learned to quilt in 1976;

Alice Allen, Virginia Avery, Elinor Peace Bailey, Marilyn Doheny, Caryl Bryer Fallert, Betty Gall, Alison Goss, Jane Hill, Lucy Koonce, Sally Lampi, Mary Mashuta, Linda McGehee, Jackie Robinson, Jean Wells, Barbara Woffard, Kaye Wood and Lynn Young for their techniques and inspiration over the years;

Also, Norm Smith with Elna, Inc.; Omnigrid, Inc.; Chapel House Fabrics; Fasco/Fabric Sales Co.; and Hoffman Fabrics.

Table of Contents

It's only natural that quilters want to wear their art on their sleeves! Over the years, this desire for personal expression in clothing has resulted in a wonderful array of what has come to be known as "Wearable Art." At any gathering of quiltmakers and quilt fanciers, you're bound to see a colorful collection of vests, jackets, and skirts—sometimes even coats—that display the skills of the quilter.

As nationally known quilted-clothing artists explore new fabrics and techniques, they develop innovative uses for classic quilting designs and materials to create wearable art. Their work provides a rich background of inspiration for stitchers who might not consider themselves artists or seamstresses, but who are eager to try their hands at creating their own art to wear.

Judy Murrah is one of those quilt artists who has made the process of making an artful patchwork garment a joyful and very successful learning experience. I met Judy at the International Quilt Market in Kansas City in 1991, shortly after I joined That Patchwork Place as managing editor. She stood out in the crowd because of the colorful patchwork jackets she wore every day as she fulfilled her duties as Director of Education for International Quilt Market. Each day, she appeared in a different jacket. From a distance, the jackets were colorful and attractive, in styles easy for anyone to wear. Up close and personal, each jacket proved to be a vibrant collage of colorful patchwork techniques created from a variety of fabrics, in true patchwork style.

Although they weren't quilted, Judy's jackets had textural appeal because so many of the patchwork pieces were made by manipulating a flat piece of fabric into a three-dimensional form. Because there is no batting in Judy's jackets, they drape attractively and have great wearing appeal, one of the things often lacking when garments are actually quilted to the lining and a layer of batting.

When I discovered that Judy had not only created each of these very wearable, very artistic jackets, but also that she was teaching classes on how to make them, I knew we had to convince her to write a book. *Jacket Jazz* is the result. In the following pages, you will find complete instructions for making five different jackets which, altogether, incorporate over thirty different patchwork techniques. This is your opportunity to learn how to create a one-of-kind, art-to-wear jacket by following a simple "recipe." As you create your jacket, patchwork piece by patchwork piece, you will learn how to create texture, movement, and color play across the surface of your work.

And, if you're like the rest of Judy's students, you won't be able to make just one jacket. You'll want to make your own version of each one of Judy's jazzy jackets. I know I do!

Barbara Weiland, Editor

When Nancy Martin asked me to do a book on my "wearable art" jackets, I hesitated. How could I possibly cram one more thing into an already impossible schedule? The voice inside came back with, "Just do it!" And so I thought, "OK, I've been teaching how to make these jackets for several years, the class handouts are all written, many of the illustrations are done, all along I've taken pictures of my students' work—what else is there to do?"

Silly girl!

Encouraged by my students' love for these jackets and my own compassion for the people who want to learn how to make my jackets but who live outside of my teaching area, I decided to stay at the computer, let the world go by, and "Just do it!" So now it's your turn to *Just do it!*

I have been teaching quilting and quilting-related classes since 1977. I loved traditional quilting, but it wasn't long before I began to embellish my quilts with linens and lace and ribbons. It was only natural to take the next step—to make jackets that combine patchwork and appliqué techniques with innovative stitching, folding, and cutting to create textured pieces from flat fabrics. In my classes, the patchwork pieces are called fabric manipulations. Pleating, tucking, blooming, and wrinkling—these are a few of the "manipulations" that add three-dimensional appeal to the surface of my jackets.

As an avid stitcher, I also love to take classes. I returned home from one very successful quilt market, my head filled with ideas based on the new techniques I had learned. I was eager to share them with my students. When I returned to the small shop in Edna, Texas, where I teach regularly, Rebbecca Matusek, the shop owner, asked me to teach a class on what I had learned. Rather than structure a class in which students only made samples of the techniques taught, I decided to organize it so that the samples could be used to create a finished jacket.

That was January 1989, and my jacket classes have been going strong ever since. During that first class, students were encouraged to make each patchwork piece and to position it wherever they wanted on the basic jacket foundation. Students struggled with this because they lacked confidence in their own design ability. It was obvious that the class would be more successful if they had a definite plan for locating each piece to create an artistically pleasing composition. This change in approach allowed each student the opportunity to be creative in the choice of materials and colors, confident that her art would, indeed, be wearable.

Now, as soon as a class "graduates," they want to know when the next jacket class will be offered. My students have become my "groupies," always eager to take the class(es) for the jacket(s) they have missed in the progression. Five jacket designs are presented in this book—and I'm hard at work on the next ones.

In all the years I've taught quilting, I've never taught anything that has had the appeal of these jacket classes. That is due in part, I believe, to the "recipe" approach that I use and that is presented in the pages that follow.

I learned many of the techniques presented here from books and from other generous quilting teachers. As I experimented with these techniques, I often developed my own variations and adaptations to achieve the desired results for my jackets. My heartfelt gratitude goes to all who have had some part in guiding me down my own path of exploration in the quilting arts. They are listed in the acknowledgments on page 3.

Teaching jacket classes has been and continues to be a source of much gratification because my students receive such wonderful compliments on their work. In some cases, students have said that the self-confidence gained through the successful completion of their jackets has changed their lives. When heads turn in restaurants and husbands and boyfriends smile proudly, I know I've succeeded far beyond my original goals. My students are proud of their work, and so am I! Several of my students have launched successful businesses, making and selling their versions of my jackets.

I'll continue to teach jacket classes as long as there are students lined up to take them. Since the demands of my job prohibit an extensive teaching/traveling schedule too far from home in Victoria, Texas, I am delighted to share my jackets with you, step by step, in the pages of this book.

Judy Murrah

Each of my loose-fitting jacket styles is based on the same basic shape with variations in the neckline treatment, jacket length, and the shaping at the bottom edge. The slightly dropped shoulder makes it easy enough for a beginner to attach the basic sleeve to an open armhole, in the same way that a sleeve is sewn to the armhole of a shirt.

Choose your favorite jacket from the styles shown below. If you are a beginner, I recommend you start with Jacket One or Five since these styles do not have a collar, making construction a bit easier. Although Jacket Three has a simple front band, the patchwork pieces are a little more complex than those in the other jackets.

♪ **NOTE:** As my students experiment with my jackets and the patchwork techniques, many of them play "mix and match," choosing their favorite style and then applying the patchwork pieces of their choice. Some of the jackets shown are a result of this "play," so they are not exactly like the pattern given here. If this approach appeals to you, you have my permission to play to your heart's content. However, I suggest that you follow one of my "recipes" for your first jacket and then as you gain skill and confidence, create your own variations, perhaps using an already-favorite jacket pattern for the foundation.

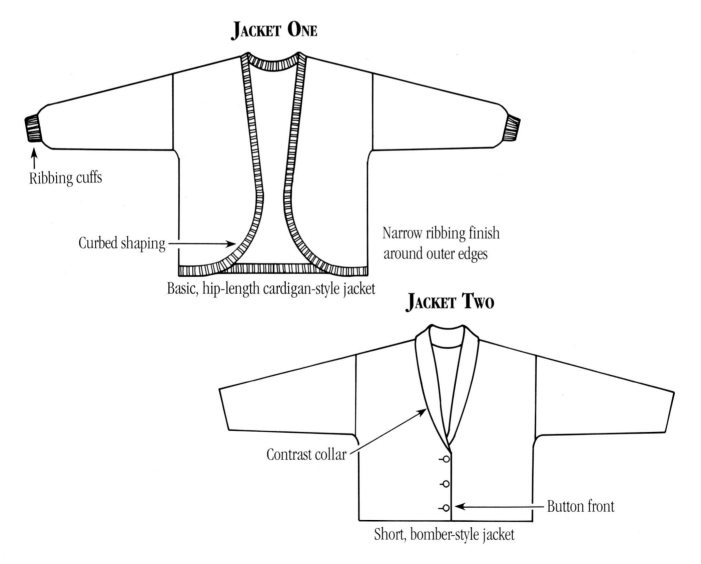

JACKET ONE

Ribbing cuffs

Curbed shaping

Narrow ribbing finish around outer edges

Basic, hip-length cardigan-style jacket

JACKET TWO

Contrast collar

Button front

Short, bomber-style jacket

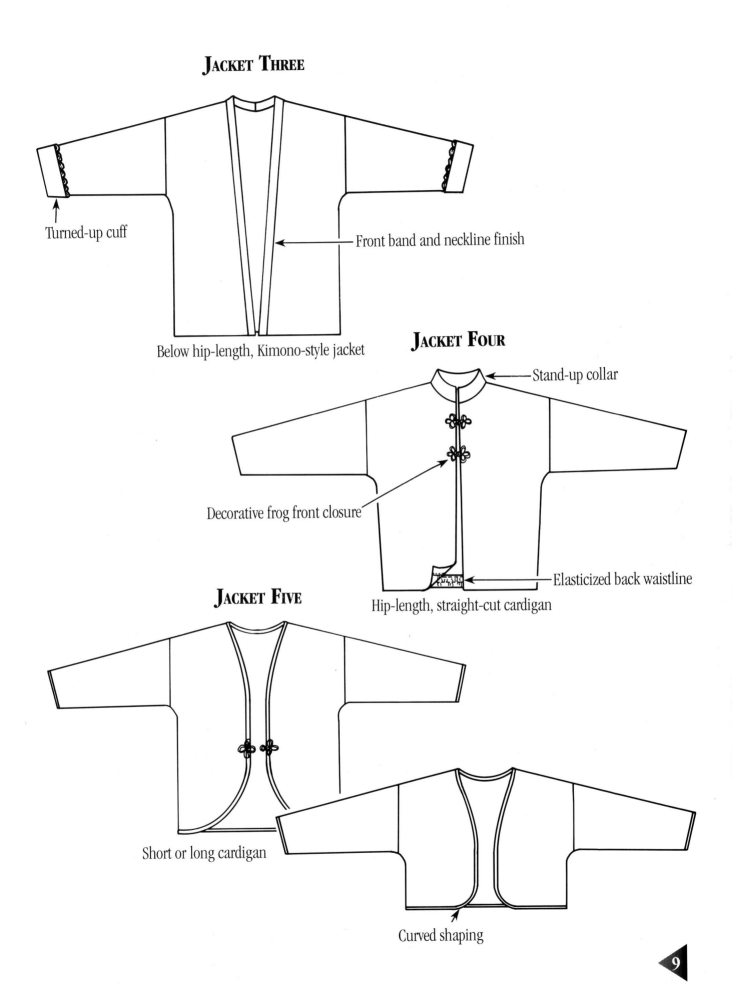

JACKET THREE

Turned-up cuff

Front band and neckline finish

Below hip-length, Kimono-style jacket

JACKET FOUR

Stand-up collar

Decorative frog front closure

Elasticized back waistline

Hip-length, straight-cut cardigan

JACKET FIVE

Short or long cardigan

Curved shaping

✓ Pattern Piece Overview

To make it possible to give patterns for the five different jackets, I started with a basic shape, then lengthened or shortened it, curved the bottom edge or left it straight, and changed the neckline treatment.

The jacket pattern pieces are printed on the pullout pattern insert at the back of the book and are multi-sized, with cutting lines marked for five sizes: Petite (6-8); Small (10-12); Medium (14-16); Large (18-20); and Extra Large (22-24). See Jacket Sizing on page 11.

To preserve the basic pattern pieces for later use, trace each pattern piece for the jacket you are making onto tracing paper, following the correct lines for your size. See special directions and illustrations below for selecting and cutting the back and front necklines.

♪ **NOTE:** All seam allowances are ½" wide.

Since five cutting lines for each jacket length would be confusing, a lengthen/shorten line is printed on the jacket front and back pattern pieces so that you can customize the pattern to a length that is comfortable on your figure. If you are petite, you will probably want to shorten the jacket front and back pattern pieces before cutting; if you are extra tall, you may want to lengthen them. Check the sleeve length, too. It has no hem allowance, just a ½" seam allowance at the bottom edge. Lengthen or shorten as needed at the double line.

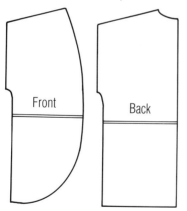

Lengthen or shorten
at double lines on
front, back, and sleeve.

The back necklines for Jackets One, Four, and Five all have the same shape so *the cutting lines for the neckline*

on the jacket back pattern piece are for Jackets One, Four, and Five only. To cut the correct back neckline shape for Jackets Two and Three, use the appropriate back neckline template (also printed on the pullout pattern insert). Position the template on the back pattern piece, aligning the center back and shoulder edges as shown. Then trace the jacket back pattern piece along the cutting lines for your size.

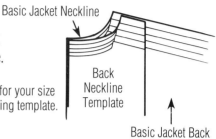

Follow cutting lines for your size
on back neckline cutting template.

The jacket front pattern piece has the neckline cutting line marked only for Jacket Four. Cutting lines for all other Jacket necklines end at the lengthen/shorten line. Five front neckline templates are given on the pattern pullout insert. Select the one for your size and position it on the jacket front pattern piece with front edges matching. Align the double line at the bottom edge of the template with the lengthen/shorten line on the pattern and make sure the cutting lines for each jacket neckline match up. Then trace the front pattern piece along the cutting lines for the jacket version you are making. Refer to the jacket front illustrations below.

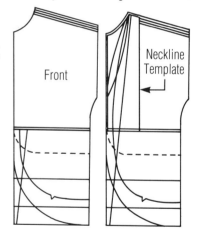

Front neckline cutting lines end
at lengthen/shorten line.

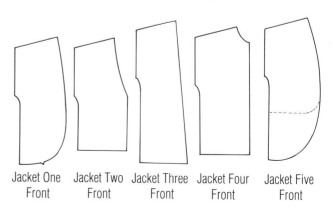

Jacket One Front   Jacket Two Front   Jacket Three Front   Jacket Four Front   Jacket Five Front

Collar pattern pieces for Jackets Two and Four are also included on the pullout pattern insert. When tracing the sleeve in your size, be sure to mark the shoulder dot and the back armhole notches for matching purposes when sewing.

Jacket Four Collar

Jacket Two Collar

seam lines. Try on to check the fit. If you feel it is too large, unpin the tissue, reposition the pieces over the master pattern and trace the next smaller size.

Jacket Sizing

This is a very loose-fitting, unstructured jacket, with lots of room in the sleeve, through the bustline, and at the full hip. You may want to use a size smaller than you're accustomed to sewing, if you prefer a closer fit. To choose your size, measure the pattern at the full hip (just above the cutting line for Jacket Two) and calculate the finished hip measurement of the size you are measuring. Compare it to your own. It should be at least 3" to 4" larger than yours for wearing ease.

After tracing the pattern pieces (front, back, and sleeve) for the jacket you are making in the selected size, cut them from the tissue and pin together along the ½"

You can also adjust the fit once the patchwork pieces have been made and attached to the jacket foundation. Simply taper the side seams from the underarm down to the bottom edge of the jacket. If you want the sleeve a little narrower at the wrist, taper the underarm seam, too.

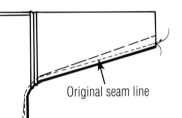

Original seam line

Taper side seams and underarm seam for a closer fit at hip and cuff.

✓Recipe for a Successful Jacket

Jacket Jazz

Making one of my jackets is a little like following a recipe. First you construct a foundation jacket, then you make and attach the patchwork pieces. Next, you embellish your work (and cover all raw edges) with a pretty trim.

Finally, you add a lining that is easy to attach and covers the wrong side of the foundation for a finished look and for wearing comfort. Follow the recipe, and the results will be a wonderful, wearable work of art.

1. Study the photos shown for each jacket and select your favorite.
2. Before you go shopping, read through "General Materials" on page 12. These are things you will need to make each of the jackets.
3. After you decide which jacket to make, refer to the "Shopping List" for that particular jacket. Assemble all your supplies and materials before you begin. (By the way, the jacket number has nothing to do with the degree of difficulty; it's just the order in which I designed and taught them.)
4. Before you start one of the jackets, read through "Jacket Construction—General Directions" on pages 14–15.

Although each jacket style requires some variation in construction, each one starts out and is put together in basically the same way.

5. Next, read through "Construction at a Glance" for the jacket you want to make. You can use this as a checklist as you work through each step. Each jacket has special finishing instructions of its own, but you will be directed to refer to the General Directions when appropriate.
6. Be sure to save the scraps from your patchwork pieces and then turn to page 85 to make a small purse to match your jacket. This little bag is great when you're "traveling light" and it makes a nice gift or bazaar item.

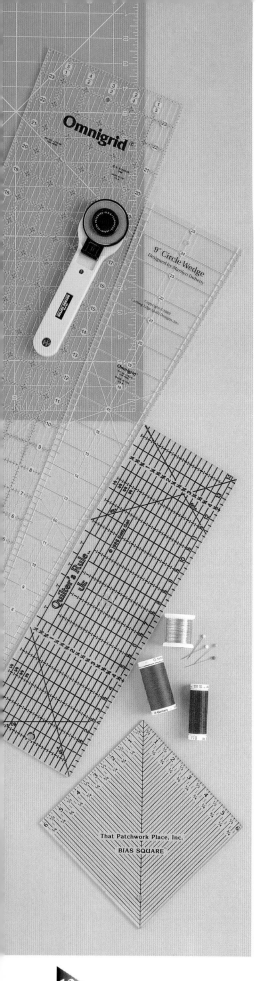

✓ General Materials

No matter which of the five featured jackets you decide to make, you will need the following materials and tools.

JACKET FABRICS

Jacket Foundation Fabric—2½ to 3 yards of cotton flannel or muslin. I use cotton flannel because I like the way the patchwork pieces cling to its napped surface and I like the way the jacket hangs when it is finished.

Jacket Lining—2½ to 3 yards silky polyester or other lightweight lining fabric. I use a silky lining fabric because it gives a more professional look and it makes the jacket easier to slip on and off.

Interfacing—⅜ to ½ yard of a lightweight fusible interfacing. This adds support and prevents stretching around the neckline and bottom edge of the jacket. Collars and bands also require interfacing. You will need a press cloth as well, and a copy of the manufacturer's fusing directions.

Large Pieces of Pattern Tracing Paper or Pattern Tracing Cloth—Trace the pattern pieces in the proper size for the jacket view you are making. Pattern pieces are on the pullout pattern insert.

Upholstery gimp, braid, bias tape, or other flat, decorative trim—You will need several yards of ½"- to ⅝"-wide trim to cover the edges of the patchwork pieces after they are attached to the jacket foundation. Check the shopping list for the jacket you are making.

Shoulder pads—I like big, thick shoulder pads to support the weight of the jacket and to minimize my hip line! Be sure to use covered, raglan-style shoulder pads, choosing a comfortable thickness for you.

Thread—in colors to match braid, lining, and fashion fabrics

Fusible web—You will need this for some of the patchwork pieces. (Check the "Shopping List" for the jacket you are making.) Choose either Wonder-Under, a web attached to a release paper, or Fine Fuse, a web without release paper that requires the use of a special Teflon press cloth.

TOOLS

Zigzag sewing machine with these optional attachments: zipper foot, gathering foot, quilting guide, tucking foot, beading/cording foot

Rotary cutter, mat, and rulers

FABRIC SELECTION FOR THE PATCHWORK PIECES

Making one of these jackets is the perfect excuse to go fabric shopping. It gives you a chance to use lots of fabrics in the colors you love. Start by choosing the jacket you want to make and study the photos for fabric ideas. Specific suggestions for fabric selection for each jacket are included in the shopping lists. Take this book to the store for reference. Yardage requirements are more than ample; you will probably have some leftovers for your fabric stash.

For easiest handling, select 100% cotton fabrics. Small amounts of other fabrics such as lamé may be used for special effects. I do not recommend prewashing the fabrics as they will lose body and will be more difficult to handle. If fabrics have been prewashed, treat them with a little spray-on starch to add body.

Following are the general guidelines for fabric selection that I share with my students in class.

1. Decide how you will wear your jacket and the mood you wish to create. Will you wear it with denim skirts and jeans for casual, everyday attire, or with a skirt or dress for work? Would you rather make it for special occasions such as holiday events? Choose fabrics that will create the desired effect.

    For casual wear, denims, solids, and calm prints are appropriate. For work or an evening out, choose some fabrics that have a touch of gold or silver in the print, plus multi-colored prints, bright solids, and blacks. For a party or holiday jacket, add some lamé fabrics. Select silkier trim with a finer texture than you might choose to mix with denim and consider trims in gold or silver as well.

2. At the fabric store, pull fabrics that match the effect you wish to create. Evaluate your selections. Is there an overall color pattern or theme? Stack the fabrics, then stand back to look at your selections. If there isn't a dominant fabric that contains many of the colors you've chosen in the other fabrics, look for one to use as the *main fabric* in your jacket.

3. Add fabrics until you have the number required. For visual interest, try to include a large print, a solid or two, small, tone-on-tone prints that look like a solid from a distance, small and medium florals or geometric prints, and a stripe or a print with a definite pattern line to follow.

4. Arrange fabrics with like colors together so they blend in a gradual transition, then evaluate. Does color flow smoothly from one fabric to the next? Remove any that stick out like a sore thumb–too bright, too dull, too light, too dark. Substitute a fabric that makes a smoother transition.

5. When you are pleased with your fabric selection, purchase the required yardage of each. Plan to use the fabric you love the most for those parts of the jacket that require the most yardage.

You can do this! And don't forget that you can add other fabrics later if something just doesn't work the way you thought it would!

✓ Jacket Care

If you must clean your finished jacket, be sure to ask the dry cleaner to clean and steam only. Pressing can ruin the beautiful textures you've so carefully created on the surface of your jacket. If you are careful to spot clean your jacket whenever necessary, dry cleaning can be kept to a minimum.

♪ **NOTE:** In the illustrations that follow, the general shape of Jacket Two will be illustrated—without the patchwork pieces. Basic construction steps are the same for the other four jacket styles.

1. The pullout pattern in this book includes the cutting lines for five different jacket styles in five different sizes. Determine which size pattern to use. Trace the appropriately sized pattern pieces for the jacket you are making onto pattern tracing paper or cloth.

2. Cut two sleeves, two fronts, and one back from both the lining and foundation fabrics. With right sides together, stitch the foundation fronts to the foundation back at the shoulder seams, *using ½"-wide seam allowances.* Press seams open. Repeat with the lining fabric.

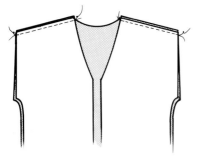

Stitch shoulder seams.

♪ **NOTE:** Pressing during the whole process of making the patchwork pieces and construction of the jacket is important. Don't skip pressing.

3. For Jackets Two and Three, sew the sleeves to the jacket *before* applying the patchwork pieces. On Jackets One, Four, and Five, attach the sleeves *after* you have applied the patchwork pieces. Press seams open. Sew the lining sleeves to the armholes; press the seam toward the sleeve. Set the lining aside.

4. Make the patchwork pieces for the jacket, *using ¼"-wide seam allowances.* In some cases, this is very important, so be sure your machine is correctly marked for an accurate ¼"-wide seam.

5. Lay the foundation flat with the right side facing up. Place the patchwork pieces on the foundation, following the specific instructions for each jacket. Each time you add a new piece, smooth out any wrinkles and pin flat. Trim each piece to fit next to the other patchwork pieces and/or even with the outside edges of the foundation. Pin securely, using lots of pins.

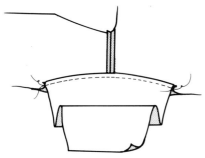

Add sleeves.

♪ **NOTE:** Anytime a part of the foundation is left showing because a patchwork piece did not cover it all, piece together any cutoff part of that patchwork piece to finish covering the foundation. If that's not possible, add more of the same fabric used in the patchwork piece to finish covering the space.

To add to the patchwork piece, place fabric right sides together with the patchwork piece and stitch through the foundation. Flip fabric to the right side, pin, and trim even with the outside edges of the foundation.

Some uncovered areas are large and call for strip piecing to cover them. To do this, use leftover strips of fabric of varying widths. Place a strip of fabric, right sides together, with the patchwork piece, sew through all three layers, and flip the strip to the right side. Continue adding strips in this manner until the area is covered.

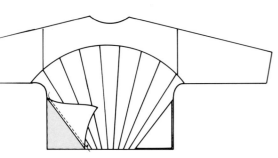

Add fabric to cover foundation.

If the area you are trying to fill is a triangular shape, piece the second side of the triangle in the same manner.

Continue strip piecing in this manner until the area is covered. Trim strip piecing even with the foundation and other patchwork pieces.

6. If you wish to add piping to the edge(s) of a completed patchwork piece, allow ¼" extra at each edge when trimming excess. Stitch the cording to the right side of the piece, then turn the seam to the wrong side and press. Use a zipper foot so you can stitch close to the corded edge.

    If you are using gimp or braid to cover the raw edges of the patchwork pieces, just butt the edges of the adjoining patchwork pieces together. Then zigzag over the raw edges to hold them in place on the jacket foundation.

    Center braid or gimp over the raw edges. If using gimp, zigzag both edges in place. If covering raw edges with a flat braid or binding, straight stitch along both edges of the trim.

    Trim the outer edges of the patchwork pieces even with the foundation and stitch in place ⅛" from the raw edges.

7. When the jacket foundation is completely covered, sew the sleeves to the jacket if you have not already done so. See step 3 on page 14. Then add gimp or braid to cover the seam line.

8. Cut 3"-wide strips of fusible interfacing and apply to the wrong side of the jacket at the center front, neckline, and bottom edges. To make straight strips fit around curved necklines, slash and spread or make tiny wedge-shaped cutouts in the interfacing as you position and fuse it in place.

9. Place completed jacket and lining wrong sides together. Check that they are the same size. Since there is so much stitching to hold the patchwork pieces in place, the jacket may now be a little smaller than the lining. Trim any excess lining even with the raw edges of the jacket.

10. With right sides together, stitch side seams, continuing to the bottom edge of the sleeve. Repeat with the lining.

11. Carefully steam press the completed jacket, being careful not to smash or rearrange any of the textures you have worked to create.

12. Follow the specific instructions for finishing each jacket.

13. Get ready for the compliments!

14. Start your next jacket.

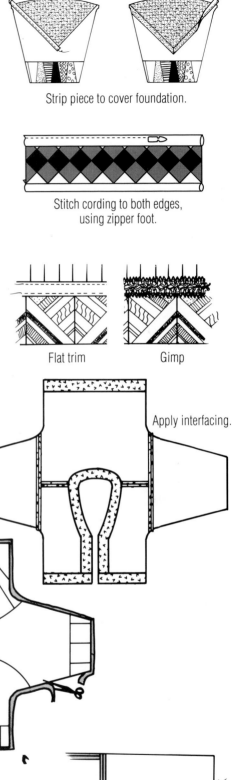

Strip piece to cover foundation.

Stitch cording to both edges, using zipper foot.

Flat trim   Gimp

Apply interfacing.

Trim away excess lining.

Stitch side and underarm seam.

Seminole Symphony

◆ **Symmetrical Bargello**

◆ **Seminole Patchwork**

◆ **Ribbon Tucking**

◆ **Blooming**

◆ **Planned Wrinkles**

◆ **Pieced Fans**

✓ *Jacket One Construction at a Glance*

1. Cut and prepare the jacket foundation and lining, following steps 1–3 on page 14. Do not attach the jacket sleeves until you have added all patchwork pieces to each sleeve.
2. Trace the pattern on page 88 for the lower center back; cut 1 piece from the fabric for the lower edge. Place the center back on the fold of the fabric and extend the cutting all the way across the fabric width at the top, curved edge of the pattern piece. *Do not cut the bottom edge yet.*

3. Make the patchwork pieces and apply to the jacket foundation, following the directions on pages 20–26.
4. Finish the foundation, following the directions on page 26.
5. Referring to the General Directions on page 15, apply the interfacing (step 8). Then sew the sleeves to the jacket and press the seams open. Cover the armhole seams with trim on the right side of the jacket. Complete step 9 on page 15.
14. Apply ribbing to sleeves and along outer raw edges of jacket, following the directions on pages 27–28.
15. Stitch the lining to the jacket, following the directions on page 28.

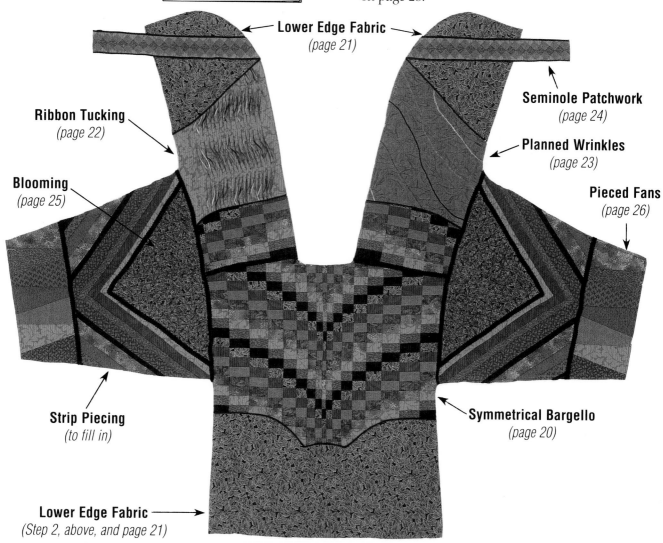

Jacket One by Roxanne Carter
Not Shown: Ribbing Neckband and Cuffs (page 27)

Shopping List

All yardage requirements listed are based on 44"-wide fabrics, unless otherwise noted. When using the same fabric for more than one patchwork technique, combine yardage requirements.

Jacket Foundation	2½ to 3 yds. cotton flannel or muslin
Jacket Lining	2½ to 3 yds. silky lining fabric
Interfacing	⅜ yd. lightweight fusible interfacing
Shoulder Pads	Covered, raglan-style shoulder pads in the thickness of your choice
Symmetrical Bargello	¼ yd. each of 8 different fabrics*
Ribbon Tucking	½ yd. fabric
	12 yds. ⅛"-wide ribbon or trim of similar width**
Planned Wrinkles	½ yd. 100% cotton fabric
	½ yd. muslin for foundation
	Decorative thread for stitching
	Assorted pieces of cording, narrow braid, ribbon, or silk crochet thread
Seminole Patchwork	⅛ yd. each of 3 different fabrics
Blooming	½ yd. each of 4 to 6 100% cotton fabrics
Pieced Fans	Leftover fabrics from other patchwork pieces
Lower Edge	½ yd. fabric that coordinates with all other fabrics
Ribbing	½ yd. 30"- to 48"-wide rib knit***
Decorative Trim	Approximately 7 yards (½" to ⅝" wide) including 1½ yds. piping for the Seminole Patchwork strips

  * A total of ¾ yd. of 8 different fabrics will make all 6 patchwork pieces.
 ** Ribbon may be an assortment of colors and textures.
*** Ribbings vary greatly in width and fiber content. Choose one with a high cotton fiber content. Avoid acrylic ribbings.

FABRIC SELECTION TIPS

- Choose the lower edge fabric first. Select a fabric that has at least three colors and then pick all other fabrics to coordinate with it. A large floral is very successful for this piece.
- Select fabrics for the Blooming that have good color penetration on both sides for a rich look. Avoid fabric with a wrong side that is white or substantially lighter than the right side since it will show when the Blooming is completed.

✓ *Symmetrical Bargello*

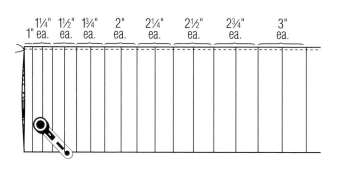

MATERIALS

¼ yd. each of 8 different fabrics

DIRECTIONS

1. Cut 3 strips, each 1½" wide, from each of 8 fabrics. Cut all strips across the fabric width. Assign each fabric a number and sew the strips together in numerical order, using ¼"-wide seams. Press all seams in one direction. The finished unit will have 3 sets of strips seamed together and should measure approximately 24" x 42".

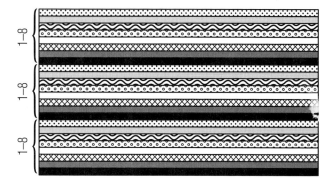

2. Fold the strip-pieced unit in half, right sides together, with the raw edges of the first and last strips matching. Stitch ¼" from edge to make one long tube. Also see step 3 and note above right.

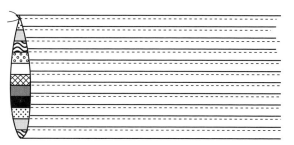

3. Using your rotary-cutting equipment, cut the tube into "rings." Make the first one 1" wide. Then cut 2 each of the following widths: 1¼", 1½", 1¾", 2", 2¼", 2½", 2¾", and 3". Continue to cut strips in sets of 2, increasing the width by ¼" each time, until you can no longer cut 2 of a given width. (Strip-piecing seams are not shown in the diagram above right for the sake of clarity.)

♪ **NOTE:** The strip-pieced tube should lie flat when folded in half in preparation for stitching. If it does not, stitch from the center out, only as far as it does lie flat. Cut strips as directed, cutting only as many as possible before you need to realign and stitch more of the tube. Each time you cut a new series of strips, first cut a new straight edge on the tube.

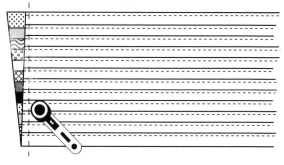

Cut away wedge to straighten edge of tube.

4. Open one seam of the 1"-wide strip at any seam line by tugging gently at each side to loosen the stitches. Place right side up on a flat surface with the seams pressed toward you. This strip will be the center of the Bargello.

5. Identify the top fabric of the 1"-wide strip. Find this same fabric in the 1¼"-wide strips; then open these 2 strips one strip down from the fabric you identified, making sure that the seams will still be pressed toward you. That means the second fabric in the 1"-wide strip will be at the top of the 1¼"-wide strips. Position 1 of these strips at each side of the center strip with top edges even. Refer to the illustration with step 7, page 21.

6. Repeat step 5 with each of the remaining sets of strips, moving down 1 strip each time you open the seam of a new strip width. Be sure that all seam allowances are pressed toward you.

7. Now double-check to make sure that the design is symmetrical on each side of the center strip.

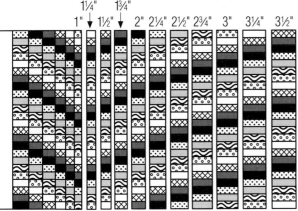

8. Pick up the strips one at a time, stacking them in order. Place a pin in the top left corner of the top strip to remind yourself that a strip will never be sewn to that edge.

9. Stitch strips together in order, using ¼"-wide seams. There is no need to pin to match the patchwork. Simply manipulate it at each seam to make it match the best you can. Your eye will see the design, not the accuracy in piecing.

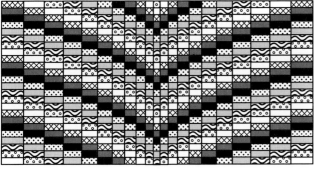

Completed Bargello

10. Lay the jacket foundation on a flat surface. Referring to the jacket layout photo on page 18 for positioning, place the completed Woven Bargello on the jacket back up to the shoulder seam and pin in place. Trim the edges even with the foundation along the shoulders and neckline. Stitch ¼" from the raw edges.

11. Place lower back piece on jacket foundation, positioning it on top of the Bargello as high or as low as you want it; pin along the top cut edge. (See jacket layout photo on page 18.) Trim any excess lower back fabric even with the bottom of the jacket. Trim excess lower back fabric even with foundation at side seams. Save pieces for lower front.

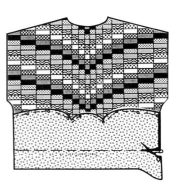

♪ **NOTE:** If you want to insert piping at the top edge of the lower back piece (and the lower front pieces, below), you will need to allow for a ¼" seam allowance at the top edge when positioning the pieces.

12. Leaving pins in at the top edge, lift the lower back fabric up out of the way; cut away excess Woven Bargello underneath, saving the pieces.

13. Place the cutaway pieces of the lower edge fabric on the lower front pieces, making sure the width at the side seams is the same on the front and back pieces so they match at the side seam edges. If the large leftovers are not wide enough to cover the fronts, strip piece scraps in place at the sides as shown. Pin in place; trim even with foundation front and bottom edges. If you want to pipe the top edges of the lower back and front pieces, remove pieces from foundation and apply piping as shown on page 15. Return pieces to foundation, pin in place, and stitch ¼" from the raw edges.

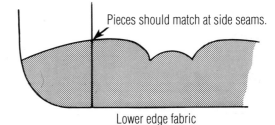

Pieces should match at side seams.

Lower edge fabric

14. Fold the leftover bargello pieces in half and cut into 2 identical pieces, shaping for the front shoulder as shown in the jacket layout photo. Add to the foundation at the front shoulder seams. The bargello designs will not match exactly at the shoulder seams, but your eye will see that the color and design are the same. Adding trim or piping here to cover the raw edges helps create the illusion that the pieces match.

✓ Ribbon Tucking

MATERIALS

18" x 30" piece of fabric
12 yds. ⅛"-wide ribbon or something similar (This may be assorted textures and colors.)

DIRECTIONS

1. *On the right side of the fabric,* make ¼"-long marks at the top and bottom edges of the rectangle (along the 18" sides). Make the first set of marks 1¾" from the raw edge and space the remaining marks 1¼" apart.

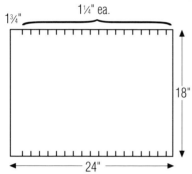

Make first set of marks 1³/₄" from the raw edge.
Space all remaining marks at 1¹/₄" intervals.

2. Place the marked rectangle *wrong side up* on the ironing board, with excess fabric away from you. Turn the right side of the fabric up to expose the first set of marks (1¾" from the edge). Fold on the marks and press to make a crisp line. Continue pressing folds along the remaining sets of marks. As you work, the newest folded edge will be nearest you and the pressed creases should be lying on top of the remaining uncreased fabric. Be careful not to "unpress" any of the creases you have already made.

3. When pressing is complete, stitch ⅜" from each fold to create a tuck. Press all tucks in one direction.

4. Divide the length of the pleated fabric into 4 equal parts. Mark by folding and pressing a crease at each division or mark with chalk.

5. Pin 1 ribbon under each tuck at the top edge of the fabric.

6. At each pressed division line, lift the tucks and turn in the opposite direction from the direction the tucks are lying above the division line. As you do this, pull each ribbon from under its tuck and twist it so it lies under the same tuck. At the next division line, reverse direction again so the ribbon is under the tuck. Pin the ribbon in place.

7. Proceed with each remaining tuck and ribbon.

8. Stitch across all tucks and ribbons, using the division lines as the sewing lines. Be sure to stitch across the top and bottom edge as well.

9. Place Ribbon Tucking on the left front. Utilize as much of this patchwork piece as possible. You may need to trim some of it away so that it fits in the empty space between the Woven Bargello and the fabric at the lower edge. If you must trim any of the ribbon-tucked fabric, channel stitch across ribbon and tucks with 2 rows of stitching, then cut between the rows of stitching. This will keep the ribbons in place. Trim even with foundation. Stitch ¼" from the raw edges.

10. If necessary, use some of the ribbon tuck fabric to cover the foundation at the underarm area.

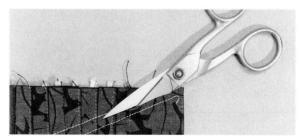

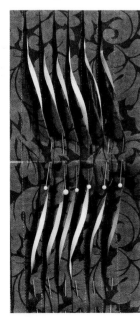 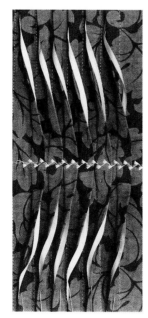

Steps 3-6   *Step 8*   *Step 9*

Planned Wrinkles

MATERIALS

16" x 20" piece of muslin for foundation
18" x 24" piece of 100% cotton fabric
Decorative thread for stitching
Assorted pieces of cording, narrow braid, ribbon, or silk
    crochet thread

DIRECTIONS

1. Immerse the 18" x 24" piece of fabric in a sink of water.
   Scrunch and then twist tightly into a ball, squeezing
   out as much water
   as possible. Secure
   the ball shape with
   a rubber band. Set
   outside to dry or dry
   in a dryer with a few
   towels to help
   absorb the water
   and speed up the
   drying.

2. When the fabric is dry, remove the rubber band and
   carefully untwist the fabric to preserve the wrinkles.
   Place the "scrunched" fabric on top of the 16" x 20"
   muslin foundation and pin to the foundation around
   the outside edges. Allow the wrinkled fabric to dictate
   the shape it takes on the flat muslin foundation.

3. Using metallic, rayon, or other special thread in the
   sewing machine, stitch wrinkled fabric to the foundation. Place cording, narrow braid, ribbon, or silk cro-
   chet yarns on top of the wrinkled fabric in random
   patterns and stitch circles, curves, straight lines, or
   zigzags to hold them in place.

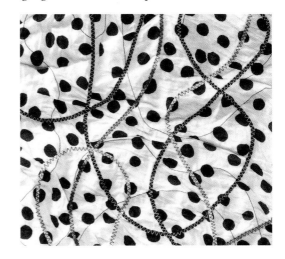

NOTE: Try stitching from the muslin side of the
fabric with ribbon floss in the bobbin for a special
look on the right side of the fabric. Check your
sewing-machine manual, a book on decorative
machine embroidery, or ask your sewing machine
dealer how to use special threads in the bobbin for
special effects on the surface of your work.

4. Place the Planned Wrinkles on the right front in the
   same way you positioned Ribbon Tucking on the left
   front, making them the same size and shape. Stitch to
   the foundation ¼" from the raw edges.

✓ *Seminole Patchwork*

MATERIALS

⅛ yd. each of 3 different fabrics

DIRECTIONS

1. Cut the following strips from the 3 fabrics selected for this patchwork piece, cutting each strip across the fabric width:

Fabric	No. of Strips	Strip Width
A	2	1½"
B	2	1¼"
C	1	1¼"

2. With right sides together, sew the strips together as shown and press all seams in one direction. The finished piece should measure approximately 5" x 42". Cut the strip-pieced unit into 1¼"-wide strips.

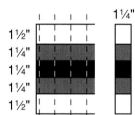

A	1½"
B	1¼"
C	1¼"
B	1¼"
A	1½"

1¼"

3. Using a ¼"-wide seam allowance, sew the strips together, offsetting each strip by 1 "square" as shown.

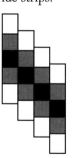

4. Using a rotary cutter and ruler, cut off the points (often called "rooftops" in my classes) on both jagged edges so there is a ¼"-wide seam allowance left beyond the corners of each square.

¼" seam allowance

2¼" wide, 36" long

5. With right sides together, sew the two short ends of the Seminole strip together to make a tube. Press the seam in the same direction as all the others.

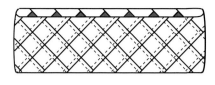

Make a straight cut through the tube as shown to open the piece into a continuous strip.

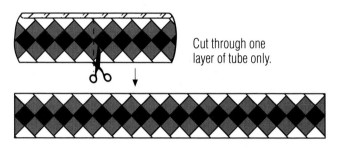

Cut through one layer of tube only.

Cut the strip in half for 2 strips of equal length.

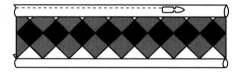

Cut strip in half.

6. With raw edges even and right sides together, stitch piping to both raw edges of each Seminole strip. Use the zipper foot so you can stitch close to the piping. Turn the seam to the wrong side and press.

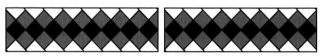

Stitch piping to both edges, using zipper foot.

7. Place a Seminole Patchwork strip diagonally on the lower right and left fronts as shown in the jacket layout photo on page 18. Pin in place. *Do not trim excess.* After the jacket side seams are sewn together, wrap the rest of the patchwork onto the jacket back. Stitch next to the cording to secure the patchwork strip to the jacket fronts and back.

✓Blooming

MATERIALS

½ yd. each of 4 to 6 different 100% cotton fabrics

DIRECTIONS

1. Cut a 16" square from each of the fabrics.
2. Decide which fabric you want to use as the bottom layer (lining) of the Blooming and set aside. Make a stack of the remaining squares in the desired order, ending with the fabric you want on top and carefully smoothing each layer in place. Be sure the fabric for the top layer has good color penetration on the wrong side.
3. Using a lead or chalk pencil and a ruler, draw parallel vertical lines on the top layer of the stack, spacing the lines as close as 1" apart or as far as 2" apart. Draw the first vertical line in the center. Continue drawing parallel vertical lines at consistent intervals.

    Create a grid by drawing horizontal lines perpendicular to the vertical lines. Draw the first one in the center and work out to the edges.

♪ **NOTE:** For maximum "blooming," draw the lines on the bias rather than the straight grain of the fabric. On some fabrics, you can follow the printed design rather than drawing lines.

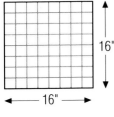 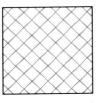

Straight-grain grid

Diagonal grid for maximum "blooming"

If you have a quilting-guide attachment for your machine, you only need to draw 1 horizontal and 1 vertical line. Then adjust the quilting guide to the desired width to stitch the additional lines.

4. With the lining piece set aside, pin the fabric layers together.
5. Stitch on each marked line. Begin in the center and work out to the edges.

6. Place the stitched fabric stack on a rotary mat. Using a rotary cutter, cut each square twice diagonally through all layers. Cut all the way into the corners of each square. Don't worry if you accidentally cut some of the stitches; you will stitch over every row again. You may need to use a small scissors to get to some of the corners.

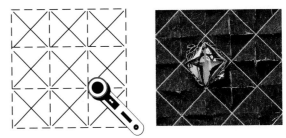

7. Position and pin the remaining fabric square (lining) on the bottom of the stack with the right side of the lining square against the wrong side of the bottom layer in the slashed piece. Stitch over each row of stitching to attach the bottom layer. You may use a decorative stitch and/or a special thread.

8. Machine wash and dry the stitched-and-cut fabric stack to make it bloom. If you want lots of "fluff" in the finished piece, dry it with jeans and/or tennis shoes. The extra friction creates more dimension.

9. Cut the Blooming in half on the diagonal. Pin each piece to a sleeve foundation with the diagonal edge at the top edge of the sleeve and the center of the piece at the shoulder mark. Anchor it to the foundation by stitching from the foundation side ¼" from the top edge of the sleeve. Trim excess Blooming even with the top edge of the sleeve.

✓ *Pieced Fans*

MATERIALS

Fabrics left over from other patchwork pieces

DIRECTIONS

1. Trace the fan on the pullout pattern insert to make a cutting template.
2. Cut 2 fans from each fabric used in your jacket. Arrange 8 to 10 fans in a pleasing order, alternating the direction of each. (For smaller jacket sizes, you will need only 8 fan pieces; for larger sizes, 9 or 10 fan pieces. Use the measurement of the bottom edge of the sleeve as a guide.) Arrange a second set of fans in a mirror image of the first.

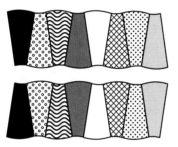

Make a mirror-image set of Pieced Fans.

3. Sew each set of fans together, using ¼"-wide seams. Press all seams in one direction.
4. Using a rotary cutter and ruler, trim one long edge of each set of pieced fans as shown. The new straight edge is the top of each strip.

5. Place a strip of pieced fans at the bottom edge of each sleeve foundation as shown in the jacket layout photo on page 18 and stitch in place at the outer edges of the sleeve. Trim excess at bottom edge and sides of Pieced Fans even with the foundation.

✓ *Finishing the Foundation*

1. Beginning at the bottom edge of the Blooming triangle on each sleeve, fill in the remaining area with strip piecing, using leftover strips of fabric or patchwork pieces. Position strips on the raw edges of the Blooming, right sides together, and stitch ¼" from the raw edge. Press toward the foundation. Continue adding strips until the foundation is covered.

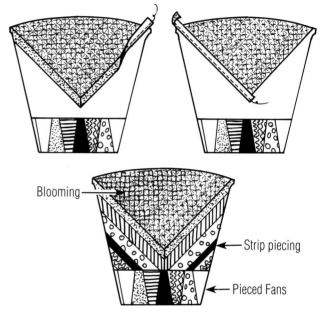

2. Finish all raw edges on the jacket and sleeves with your choice of gimp, braid, or bias binding as shown on page 15.
3. Sew the sleeves to the jacket armhole and press the seam open. Cover the completed seam line with the desired trim. Complete steps 8 and 9 on page 15.
4. With right sides together, stitch the underarm seam of the jacket and sleeve. Press seam open. Repeat with the lining.

✓Ribbing

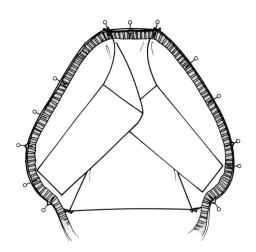

1. Cut ribbing into enough 3"-wide strips to make the length given in the chart below for the jacket size you are making. Piece as necessary, being careful not to stretch the ribbing. Press piecing seams open.

Size	Ribbing Length
Ex. Small	86"
Small	92"
Medium	100"
Large	108"
Ex. Large	116"

2. Fold ribbing in half lengthwise, with wrong sides together and raw edges even.

3. Fold the length of ribbing in half and mark the fold with a pin to designate neckline center back (CB). Then place a pin on each side of the center-back pin to mark the shoulder location, spacing each pin the distance indicated for the size you are making.

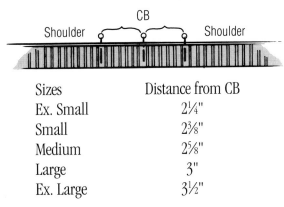

Sizes	Distance from CB
Ex. Small	2¼"
Small	2⅜"
Medium	2⅝"
Large	3"
Ex. Large	3½"

4. Mark the center back at the jacket neckline and at the bottom edge with pins.

5. Pin the ribbing to the right side of the jacket back neckline with raw edges even, matching pins in the ribbing to the center back and to the shoulder seams.

6. Pin the ribbing from the shoulder seam to the first notch, using a 1:1 ratio. In other words, do not stretch the ribbing. Make sure both the ribbing and the garment lie flat in this area.

7. Continue pinning approximately 12½" of the ribbing around the front curve between the first and second notches, easing ribbing without creating gathers or puckers.

8. Pin ribbing to one-half of the lower edge of the jacket from the notch to the center back in a 1:1 ratio. Trim excess ribbing, leaving a ¼"-wide seam allowance at center back. Repeat with the remaining ribbing on the other half of the jacket.

9. Open out the ribbing and stitch ends, right sides together. Press seam open. Refold the ribbing and pin to the bottom edge of jacket, matching the center back seam in the ribbing to the center back of the jacket.

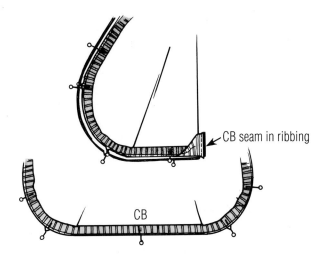

CB seam in ribbing

CB

10. Using a ¼"-wide seam allowance, stitch the ribbing to the jacket.

11. For cuffs, cut 2 strips of ribbing, each 5½" wide and the length of your wrist measurement plus ½".

12. With right sides together, stitch the short ends of each cuff, using a ¼"-wide seam allowance. Finger press seam open.

13. Fold ribbing cuff in half, with wrong sides together and raw edges even. Divide each cuff into fourths and mark with pins. Divide and mark the lower edge of each sleeve the same way.

14. Pin cuffs to sleeves, matching the pins and having raw edges even. With ribbing on top, stitch ¼" from the raw edge, stretching the ribbing to fit.

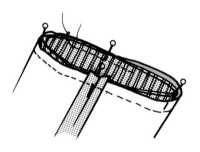

✓Lining

1. With right sides together, stitch the lining to the jacket, leaving an 8"-long opening at the bottom edge at the center back for turning. Trim seam to ¼". Turn right side out and press.

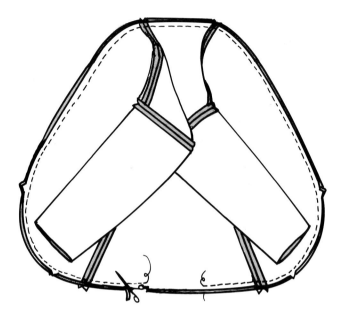

2. Slipstitch lining in place over raw edges of jacket and ribbing.

Lining

3. Press under the seam allowance at the bottom edge of each lining sleeve. Slipstitch lining in place over the raw edges of the sleeve and ribbing.

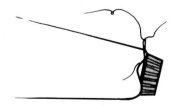

4. Tack shoulder pads in place on inside of jacket.

Jacket One by Judy Murrah, Victoria, Texas. High-contrast yellow and black paired with cool, complementary purples and blue-greens add mystery and illusion to this cardigan-styled jacket. Ribbon Tucking and Planned Wrinkles add textural appeal.

Striking Symmetrical Bargello illustrates the use of the yellow accent to create maximum pattern rhythm.

Magic Melody

- ▼ **Wonder Wedge**
- ▼ **Magic Maze**
- ▼ **Revised Reverse Appliqué**
- ▼ **Mock Smock**

- ▼ **Machine Grid Smocking**
- ▼ **Shirring**
- ▼ **Prairie Points**
- ▼ **Weirdo Yo-Yo**

1. Cut and prepare the jacket foundation and lining, following steps 1–3 on page 14.

2. Using the collar pattern for Jacket Two, cut 2 collars from the collar fabric and 1 from the interfacing.

3. Apply interfacing to the wrong side of 1 collar, following manufacturer's directions. Set collar pieces aside.

4. Make the patchwork pieces and apply to the jacket foundation, following the directions on pages 34–41.

5. Finish the jacket foundation, following the directions on page 41.

6. Following the directions on page 15, apply the interfacing (step 8) and then complete step 9.

7. Stitch 1 collar to the lining and 1 to the jacket, following the directions on page 41.

8. Finish the jacket, following the directions on page 42.

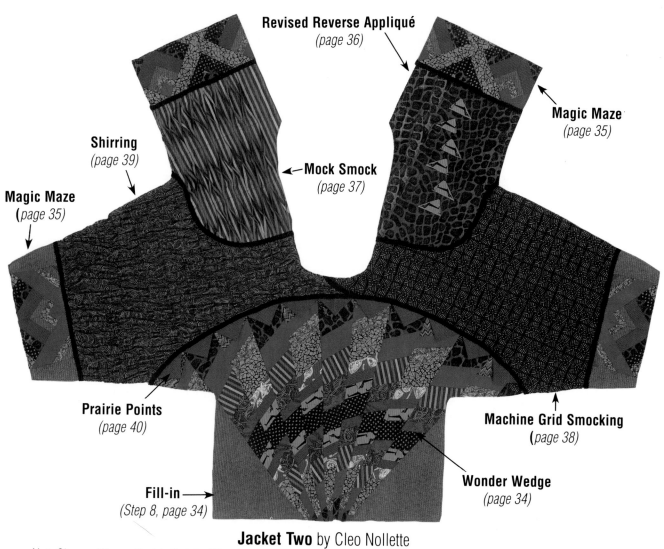

Revised Reverse Appliqué
(page 36)

Magic Maze
(page 35)

Shirring
(page 39)

Mock Smock
(page 37)

Magic Maze
(page 35)

Prairie Points
(page 40)

Machine Grid Smocking
(page 38)

Wonder Wedge
(page 34)

Fill-in
(Step 8, page 34)

Jacket Two by Cleo Nollette

Not Shown: Woven Prairie Points (Step 5, page 40, and Step 6, page 42), Weirdo Yo-Yo (page 41), Collar (page 41)

Shopping List

All yardage requirements listed are based on 44"-wide fabrics, unless otherwise noted. When using the same fabric in more than one patchwork piece, combine the yardage requirements.

Jacket Foundation	2½ to 3 yds. cotton flannel or muslin
Jacket Lining	2½ to 3 yds. silky lining fabric
Interfacing	½ yd. lightweight fusible interfacing
Shoulder Pads	Covered, raglan-style shoulder pads in the thickness of your choice
Wonder Wedge	⅛ yd. each of 13 different fabrics
Magic Maze	⅛ yd. each of 7 different high-contrast fabrics
Revised Reverse Appliqué	½ yd. each of 2 different fabrics
	½ yd. Fine Fuse (and a Teflon press cloth) or ½ yd. Wonder-Under
Mock Smock	½ yd. fabric with a uniformly spaced stripe
Machine Grid Smocking	½ yd. fabric
Shirring	1 yd. printed fabric
Prairie Points	⅛ yd. each of 3 different fabrics
Weirdo Yo-Yo	Scraps from other patchwork pieces
Collar	⅓ yd. fabric
Embellishment	Decorative buttons, beads
Decorative Trim	Approximately 8 yds. (½" to ⅝" wide)

In addition to the fabrics listed, you will need the following special supplies:
  Gathering foot for your sewing machine
  9° Circle Wedge Ruler
Optional:
  8" square ruler to use with rotary cutter

FABRIC SELECTION TIPS

- First decide on the overall feeling you want in your finished jacket and establish a color theme. You will need 14 different fabrics for this jacket.

- Select the striped fabric for Mock Smock on the jacket left front and then choose the remaining fabrics for the jacket. If you wait to select the striped fabric after selecting all others, it will be more difficult to find one that works.

- For the Wonder Wedge on the jacket back, choose a favorite fabric that fits your color theme, and then select 12 additional coordinating fabrics.

- Remember that one sleeve will be covered with Shirring and the other with Machine Grid Smocking. Fabrics for these two large areas should complement each other, and they should be selected from the fabrics you've chosen for the Wonder Wedge.

- Pay special attention to balancing the colors in Revised Reverse Appliqué with the striped fabric in Mock Smock and the fabrics chosen for the sleeves.

- A solid-colored fabric works well for the collar and is a nice backdrop for the Prairie Points.

✓ Wonder Wedge

This patchwork piece is made using Marilyn Doheny's innovative 9° Circle Wedge Ruler. This exercise represents only the tip of the iceberg when it comes to the designs that can be created using this unique cutting guide.

MATERIALS

⅛ yd. each of 13 different fabrics

DIRECTIONS

1. Cut a strip from each of the 13 fabrics, varying the cut widths from 1½" to 3" for interest. Cut each strip across the fabric width, selvage to selvage.
2. Arrange strips with like colors together and blending into the next color. The 2 strips in the center of your arrangement will be the most prominent in the finished piece, so plan accordingly.
3. When you are pleased with the arrangement, sew the strips together, using ¼"-wide seams. Press all seams in one direction. The finished piece should measure approximately 22" x 42".
4. Using the 9° ruler, cut nine 60° wedges (or ten for larger sizes). Position the wedge-shaped ruler with the wide end up on the pieced fabric and the 60° mark parallel to the seam lines. Cut the first wedge.
5. Turn the ruler so the narrow end is up, align the 60° mark as before, and cut the next wedge. Continue alternating the direction of the ruler and cutting wedges until you have cut the required number of wedges. You may want to save the leftover triangles for steps 7 and 8.

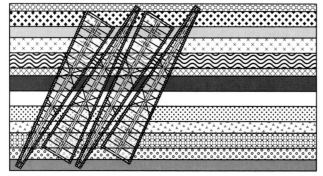

Align wedge on 60° mark.

♪ NOTE: The 60° mark will not hit in the same place on the strip-pieced unit for the large end and the small end of the ruler. However, it is important to always line it up in the same location for all cuts made with the wide end up and those made with the short end up. That way, you will have 2 sets of matching wedges.

6. Sew the wedges together, using ¼"-wide seams and alternating the wedge orientations. It helps to pin wedges together at the top and bottom of each seam. Press all seams in one direction.
7. Position the completed Wonder Wedge on the jacket back with the narrow end toward the bottom edge as shown in the jacket layout photo on page 32. A small amount of the wedge should extend below the bottom edge of the jacket. Pin in place. Trim. You will probably need to add partial wedge segments cut from the leftovers to each outer edge of the wedge to fill in the foundation down to the underarm seam.
8. Cover the exposed jacket foundation on each side of the Wonder Wedge with a piece of fabric cut to fit. A darker-toned fabric is more slimming here. If you prefer, you may use the triangles that were left from cutting the wedges. Matching up the pattern of the leftovers with the fan, pin the leftover in place on the foundation, aligning the raw edges of the foundation with the raw edges of the wedge. Stitch ¼" from the raw edge. Press and trim to complete the fan shape.

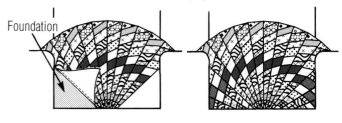

Fill in with fabric pieces
OR
with wedge leftovers.

✓ *Magic Maze*

MATERIALS

⅛ yd. each of 7 high-contrast fabrics

DIRECTIONS

1. Cut a strip from each of the 7 fabrics, varying the widths and cutting each one across the fabric width. When sewn together, the resulting strip should be 8" wide.
2. Sew the strips together, using ¼"-wide seams. Strips 1 and 7 will be the most prominent in this piece, so plan accordingly. Press all seams in one direction.
3. Cut the strip-pieced unit into five 8" squares. If strip-pieced unit is a little narrower or wider (up to 8½"), cut squares that are a little larger or smaller than 8".

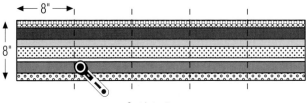

Cut into 5 squares.

4. Cut each square twice diagonally to yield 4 triangles. (A, B, C, and D).

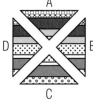

5. Lay out 2 rows of 5 squares (10 triangles) as shown.

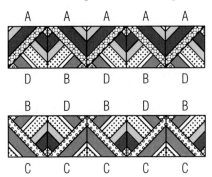

6. Decide which of the two designs you want for the jacket center fronts and which design you want for the sleeve bands. Then move one of the "sleeve" blocks to the end of the layout you have chosen for the jacket fronts as

shown. Half of this block will not match the rest of the layout, but that is not a concern because most of it will be cut off at the side seam.

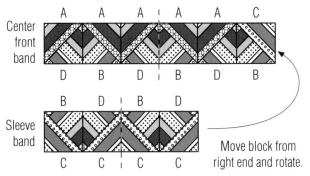

Move block from right end and rotate.

7. Now assemble the triangles into blocks and stitch the blocks together so that you have 2 sets of 3 blocks for each jacket front and 2 sets of 2 blocks for each sleeve.

For jacket front

For sleeves

8. Position the completed Magic Maze strips on the jacket fronts and sleeves at the lower edges as shown in the jacket layout photo on page 32. Stitch ¼" from raw edges.
9. Piece another fabric strip to each end of the Magic Maze on each sleeve to cover the foundation. Position each strip right side down on the sleeve, aligning raw edges with the Magic Maze, and stitch, using a ¼"-wide seam. Press and trim edges even with the sleeve foundation. Stitch ¼" from raw edges.

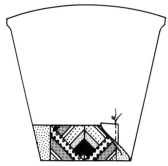

Add fabric pieces to cover foundation.

✓ Revised Reverse Appliqué

MATERIALS

½ yd. each of 2 different fabrics
18" square of Fine Fuse (and a Teflon press cloth) or
Wonder-Under

DIRECTIONS

1. Cut an 18" square from each fabric.
2. Apply Wonder-Under or Fine Fuse to the wrong side of the fabric that you want on top. Follow the manufacturer's directions. If you use Wonder-Under, remove the protective paper backing after applying it to the fabric.

♪ **NOTE:** Final fusing will be done in step 6.

3. Layer the two fabrics so the *right side of the bottom fabric is against the wrong side of the top fabric.* Pin.
4. Using thread in a color that contrasts with the top layer of fabric, machine stitch any pattern you desire. You can either draw shapes or patterns on the top fabric or you can follow an existing pattern in the fabric (either the top or bottom fabric). Alternatively, make shapes such as hearts, triangles, or diamonds in a random pattern. Make single or double rows of stitching, as much or as little as you wish. Experiment with ribbon floss or other decorative thread in the bobbin and stitch from the wrong side. Examine the photos of Jacket Two on pages 32 and 43 for additional ideas.
5. When satisfied with your stitching, cut away the top layer of fabric inside the stitched shapes so the bottom fabric shows through. Be sure to trim close to the stitching.

6. When trimming is completed, fuse the two layers by pressing them together.

♪ **NOTE:** To maintain design options, you may not wish to complete the fusing until after the appliqué piece is positioned on the jacket foundation. You may decide you want to do more stitching and cutting before you fuse and attach this piece to the foundation permanently.

7. Pin the Revised Reverse Appliqué piece to the right jacket front just above the Magic Maze as shown in the jacket layout photo on page 32. Trim even with foundation along side seam and underarm.

✓ *Mock Smock*

MATERIALS

½ yd. fabric with uniformly spaced vertical stripes (1"- to 2"-wide striped designs are the easiest to handle in this patchwork piece, although you can experiment with other vertically oriented designs, including plaids, for unusual and different effects.)

DIRECTIONS

1. Leaving a 1" width of fabric flat on the left-hand edge of the piece and a 3" width flat on the right-hand edge, fold, pin, and press uniformly sized box pleats across the width of the fabric. Fold and press along the edge of every other stripe in opposite directions. This will form a box pleat on the right side and tucks of an equal depth on the wrong side.

2. Measure down and mark every 3" on each pleat. Stitch across the pleats at the top and bottom edges and every 6" in between, being careful not to twist the edges of the pleats as you stitch across them. Use pins to mark the midpoint between the rows of stitching on each pleat.

3. Pinch each box pleat together at its midpoint (the first 3" marking) and secure with machine or hand bar tacking.

   To secure pleats by hand, thread a needle with a double strand of sewing thread. Knot. Insert the needle from the wrong side and make 3 stitches in the same place. Move to the next "pinch" location by carrying the thread horizontally across the *wrong side* of the work. Tack as before and continue in the same manner across the piece until it measures the width of the left front, including a 3"-wide area on the remaining edge that is untucked.

4. Pin the Mock Smock to the left jacket front just above the Magic Maze as shown in the jacket layout photo on page 32. Trim edges even with underarm seam.

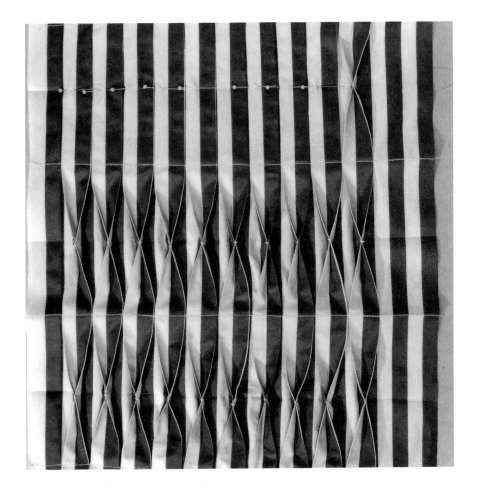

✓ *Machine Grid Smocking*

MATERIALS

¾ yd. fabric

DIRECTIONS

1. Start with a piece of fabric that measures approximately 20" x 42".
2. On the wrong side of the fabric, draw a grid of vertical and horizontal lines spaced 1" apart.
3. Set your sewing machine for an ¼"-wide zigzag stitch and set the stitch width at 0 or the shortest stitch length available. It may be necessary on some machines to lower the feed dog to achieve this. Or, set your machine for ¼"-wide bar tacking.
4. Thread the machine with regular or decorative thread in a contrasting color.
5. With the wrong side of the fabric facing up, fold along the first vertical line, but do not press a crease. At the first horizontal line intersection, bar tack over the folded edge or make approximately 7 zigzag stitches. Without cutting the thread, move down to the next cross mark and stitch in the same manner. Continue down the line until all cross marks are stitched.
6. Fold along the second line. Tack as described above, but position the stitching halfway between the grid intersections. To make spacing consistent, place the back end of the presser foot at the last drawn line.

7. Repeat steps 5 and 6, alternating across the remainder of the fabric.
8. Working from the right side, pull the fabric so the thread tacks show.
9. Position the completed Machine Grid Smocking on the right sleeve, placing it above the Wonder Wedge and allowing it to extend into the right front and across the right back neckline as shown in the jacket layout photo on page 32 and in the illustration below. It should cover the entire right sleeve and shoulder. Trim it to expose all of Wonder Wedge on the jacket back. Cut in an arc to expose as much as possible of the Revised Reverse Appliqué on the front. Pin in place. Trim outer edges even with foundation and stitch ¼" from the raw edges.

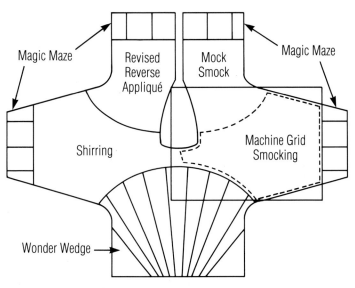

Dashed lines indicate cutting lines.

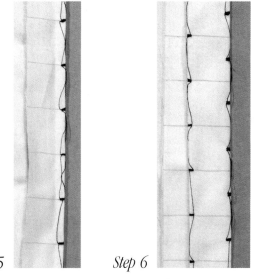

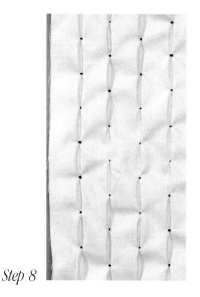

Step 5   *Step 6*   *Step 8*

✔ *Shirring*

MATERIALS

1 yd. printed fabric

DIRECTIONS

1. On the wrong side of the fabric, draw parallel lines spaced 1" apart across the width or length of the fabric. On some fabrics, you can follow the pattern on the fabric to draw the lines. If you use a quilting guide on your machine, it is not necessary to draw these lines.
2. Attach the gathering foot to your machine. Set the stitch length as long and the tension as tight as the machine allows. Practice stitching on a scrap of fabric and adjust if necessary so that the piece of gathered fabric is approximately ⅓ to ½ smaller than it was originally. If your machine is gathering too tightly, shorten the stitch and decrease the tension a notch or two and test again.
3. When you are pleased with the results, stitch on the lines drawn on the yard of fabric. After stitching the first line, stitch the remaining lines more slowly, taking time to smooth the fabric in front of the gathering foot as you stitch to avoid bunching and puckering.

♪ **NOTE:** If you want more gathering, you can stitch across the first row of gathers. Working from the wrong side of the fabric, eyeball parallel gathering lines (spaced 1" apart as before) that cross the gathered lines. Stitch. After the fabric has been gathered in one direction, it is bulkier and the second gathering will not be as full as the first. If desired, you may be able to compensate for this difference by increasing the stitch length and tension for the cross-gathered rows of stitching.

Because gathering created with the gathering foot is secured in the stitches, the resulting shirred fabric can be cut and trimmed to any size or shape.

4. Position the completed Shirring on the left sleeve as shown in the jacket layout photo on page 32. Cut to fit in a shape that matches the Machine Grid Smocking on the right half of the jacket. Join the Machine Grid Smocking and the Shirring at an angle at the center back neck edge as shown in the photo. Trim outer edges even with foundation and stitch ¼" from the raw edges.

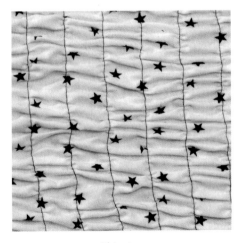

Shirring

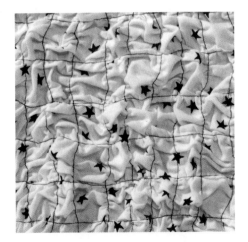

Cross Shirring

✓ *Prairie Points*

MATERIALS

⅛ yd. each of 3 different fabrics

DIRECTIONS

1. Cut a 4½"-wide strip from each of 3 fabrics, cutting across the fabric width.
2. On the wrong side of the lightest color strip, mark a line ½" from the long cut edge.
3. Layer the 3 fabric strips with wrong sides facing up and the marked strip on top. Using a rotary cutter and ruler, make vertical cuts, spaced every 4" through all layers, ending each cut at the marked line on the top fabric strip. Separate the strips and set aside one piece to use for single Prairie Points on the jacket back.

4. Fold down a corner, with wrong sides together, on each of the sections on the 2 remaining strips and press, folding the 2 strips in opposite directions as shown.

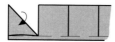

For "Woven Prairie Points," fold in opposite directions.

Then fold down a corner again to complete each point.

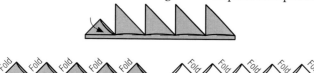

5. To weave the 2 strips together, layer them on a flat surface with the folded sides facing up and with the upper strip offset slightly to the right. Only two sets of points will be shown in the following illustrations.

Open out the first fold in each strip as shown.

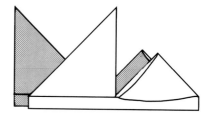

Fold the point of lower strip down over upper strip.

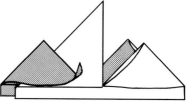

Then, fold the upper point down.

Continue in this manner with each set of points to complete the woven strip.

Carefully slide the top layer to the right to center the points along the length of the strip. Pin the layers together, then stitch close to the bottom of the triangles to catch the raw edges. Use a short stitch length. Set the Woven Prairie Points aside until the jacket is completed. Then stitch the strip to the underside of the completed collar as shown in step 5 on page 42.

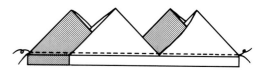

6. Fold and press Prairie Points on the remaining strip as described in step 4. (Direction does not matter.) Stitch to catch the raw edges as shown in step 5. Trim seam allowance to ¼".
7. Position the single band of Prairie Points along the top edge of the Wonder Wedge on the jacket back, positioning the points in the center of each wedge as shown in the jacket layout photo on page 32.

✓Weirdo Yo-Yo

MATERIALS

Leftovers from the previous patchwork pieces

DIRECTIONS

1. Make a template, using the Yo-Yo pattern below. Use the pattern to cut several circles from the leftover patchwork pieces. Be sure that at least 2 fabrics are within each circle you cut.
2. Thread a needle with double thread and knot the ends together. Turn under ⅛" at the edge of each circle and do a running stitch very close to the folded edge. Draw thread up as tightly as possible to form a Yo-Yo and backstitch to secure. Push the needle through to the back and knot the thread end to secure. The gathered side is the right side of the completed Yo-Yo.

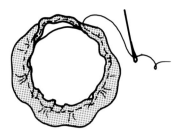

3. After finishing the jacket foundation, arrange the Yo-Yos on the jacket front, adding decorative buttons. Blindstitch or feather stitch each Yo-Yo in place around the outside edge. Or, sew several to the collar in a cluster and add beads, charms, or buttons.

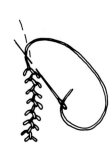

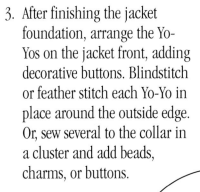

Weirdo Yo-Yos
Pattern

✓Finishing the Foundation

1. Finish all raw edges on the jacket and sleeves with your choice of gimp, braid, or bias binding as shown on page 15.
2. Complete steps 8 and 9 on page 15.
3. With right sides together, stitch the continuous underarm seam of the jacket and sleeve as shown on page 15. Press the seam open.

✓Collar

1. If you have not already done so, complete steps 2 and 3 under Jacket Two Construction at a Glance, page 32.
2. Pin the interfaced collar to the neckline of the completed jacket foundation with right sides together, matching center fronts and center back and clipping the back neckline as necessary for a smooth fit. Stitch ½" from the raw edges. Trim the seam to ¼" and press the seam toward the collar. Repeat with the remaining collar and the lining.

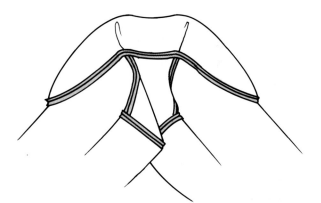

✓Finishing

1. Press under ¼" at the bottom edge of the sleeve lining.
2. With right sides together, pin the jacket/collar unit to the lining/collar unit. Stitch, leaving an 8"-long opening at the center back of the jacket bottom edge for turning. Clip curves and trim seams to ¼". Turn right side out, pushing lining sleeves into the jacket sleeves.

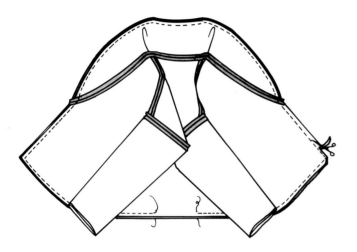

3. Turn in the seam allowances at the opening left for turning at the bottom edge of the jacket. Slipstitch the opening closed.

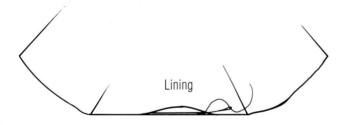

Lining

4. To anchor lining to jacket at neckline, hand or machine stitch in the ditch in the neckline seams.

5. Slipstitch the edges of the sleeve and lining sleeve together by hand, or machine edgestitch together.

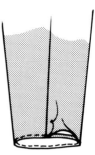

6. Turn up ¼" along the raw edge of the Woven Prairie Points; press and stitch.

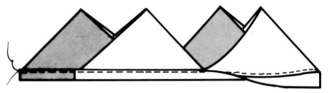

Position Prairie Points on the underside of the collar along the outer edge. Remove any extra Prairie Points. Hand or machine stitch in place.

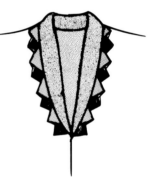

7. Add buttons and buttonholes to the fronts, if desired.
8. Tack shoulder pads in place on inside of jacket.

Jacket Two by Nancy J. Martin, Woodinville, Washington. Nancy used theme fabric to personalize her jacket. The placement of the cup and saucer motif under the teapot created the perfect area for decorative stitching in multi-colored metallics. Personalized collar embellishments and the feminine color scheme announce, "It's Tea Time!"

Jacket Two by Pat Creech, Houston, Texas. Large, medium, and small prints effectively combine to showcase the fabric manipulations and patchwork. A solid-colored collar provides a backdrop for the Woven Prairie Points.

Bargello Rhapsody

- Rhapsody Bargello
- Prissy Puffing
- Spiral Bias
- Zigzag Strata
- Flying Geese

- Elinor's Fan
- Quilting Crumbs
- Striking Stripes
- Flat Biscuits
- Rose Petal Trim

1. Cut and prepare the jacket foundation and lining, following steps 1–3 on page 14.
2. From the fabric for the neck/front band, cut 2 strips, each 3½" wide, cutting across the fabric width.
3. Decide how wide you want the turned-up cuff at the bottom edge of the sleeves. Cut a fabric strip of the desired width for each sleeve. Position on the sleeve foundation. Pin and stitch in place ¼" from raw edges.
4. Make the patchwork pieces and apply to the jacket foundation, following the directions on pages 48–54.
5. Finish the jacket foundation, following the directions on page 55.
6. Following the directions on page 15, apply the interfacing (step 8) and then complete step 9.
7. Apply the neck/front band as shown on page 55.
8. Stitch the lining to the jacket, following the directions on pages 55–56.
9. Add Rose Petal Trim to finish the bottom edge of each sleeve as shown on page 56. Turn cuff up, exposing the sleeve lining.

♪ **NOTE:** If you do not want the lining fabric to be exposed on the outside of the cuff, you must stitch another piece of fabric to the bottom edge of the sleeve lining before assembling the lining. Cut the fabric strip for each sleeve 3" wider than the desired cuff width and turn under ¼" at the top edge. Edgestitch to the right side of the sleeve lining and cut away lining underneath.

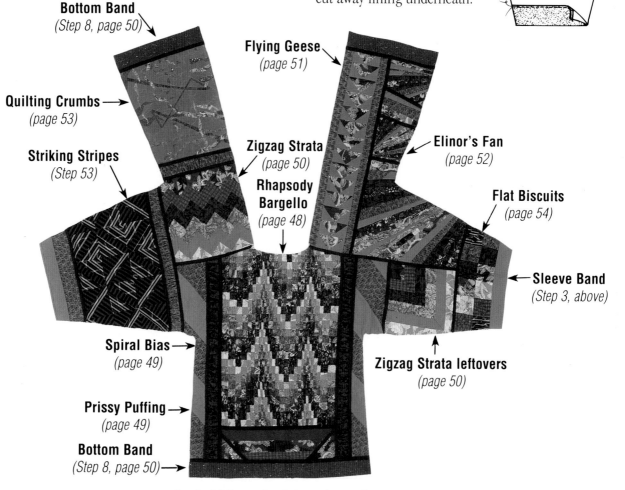

Bottom Band
(Step 8, page 50)

Flying Geese
(page 51)

Quilting Crumbs
(page 53)

Striking Stripes
(Step 53)

Zigzag Strata
(page 50)

Rhapsody Bargello
(page 48)

Elinor's Fan
(page 52)

Flat Biscuits
(page 54)

Sleeve Band
(Step 3, above)

Spiral Bias
(page 49)

Zigzag Strata leftovers
(page 50)

Prissy Puffing
(page 49)

Bottom Band
(Step 8, page 50)

Jacket Three by Joanne Lauterjung
Not Shown: Rose Petal Trim (page 54), Neck/Front Band (page 55)

 Shopping List

All yardage requirements listed are based on 44"-wide fabrics, unless otherwise noted. When using the same fabric in more than one patchwork piece, combine the yardage requirements.

Jacket Foundation	2½ to 3 yds. cotton flannel or muslin
Jacket Lining	2½ to 3 yds. silky lining fabric
Interfacing	½ yd. lightweight fusible interfacing
Shoulder Pads	Covered, raglan-style pads in the thickness of your choice
Rhapsody Bargello	¼ yd. each of 8 different fabrics
Prissy Puffing	¼ yd. fabric
Spiral Bias	⅛ yd. each of 2 different fabrics
Zigzag Strata	7 strips, each 2" wide, cut across the fabric width (Choose a combination of dark and light colors.)
Flying Geese	¼ yd. fabric for main triangles
	¼ yd. fabric for background triangles
Elinor's Fan	13" x 20" muslin foundation
	Assorted fabric strips (none wider than 2") cut from leftover fabrics
Quilting Crumbs	⅓ yd. background fabric
	⅓ yd. fine tulle netting in a dark color
	⅓ yd. Fine Fuse (and a Teflon press cloth) or ⅓ yd. Wonder-Under
	Snips, strips, and threads from the patchwork pieces for this jacket
Striking Stripes	⅓ yd. each of 2 different striped fabrics
Flat Biscuits	⅛ yd. muslin or other plain fabric
	Twelve 4" squares of 2 to 6 different fabrics left over from other patchwork pieces
Rose Petal Trim	¼ yd. fabric
Neck/Front Band	¼ yd. fabric
Decorative Trim	Approximately 8–10 yds. (½" to ⅝" wide)

In addition to the fabrics listed, you will need the following special supplies:
Gathering foot for your sewing machine
Optional:
    4½"-wide ruler to use with rotary cutter

FABRIC SELECTION TIPS

- Choose at least eight to ten different fabrics. Since it is usually more difficult to find striped fabrics for the Striking Stripes after you've chosen all the other fabrics, find two striped fabrics *first*.
- Next, select fabrics for Prissy Puffing, Flying Geese, Quilting Crumbs background, and the fabric for the sleeve and front bands.
- Choose all remaining fabrics to coordinate with these.

✓*Rhapsody Bargello*

MATERIALS

¼ yd. each of 8 different fabrics

DIRECTIONS

1. Choose 1 of the 8 fabrics as the "accent" color (#1) and then plan the arrangement of the remaining fabrics so that the colors blend in a natural progression, assigning them numbers 2–8.
2. Cut 3 strips, each 1½" wide, from each of the 8 fabrics. You should have a total of 24 strips. Cut all strips across the fabric width.
3. Sew the strips together in numerical order, using ¼"-wide seams. Make 3 identical strip-pieced units, then sew the 3 units together as shown. Press all seams toward the accent fabric. The finished piece of 24 strips should measure approximately 24" x 40".

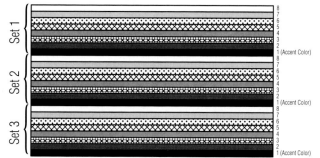

4. With right sides together, sew the first and last strip together to make a tube and press the seam in the same direction as all other seams. Using your rotary-cutting equipment, cut the tube into the number of strips ("rings") indicated in the widths given below.

Strip	No. of Strips	Strip Width
A	5	1¼"
B	9	1"
C	11	¾"

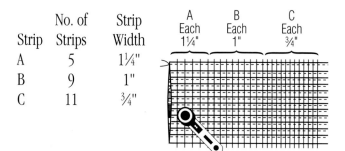

A Each 1¼" B Each 1" C Each ¾"

♪ **NOTE:** The strip-pieced tube should lie flat when folded in half in preparation for stitching. If it does not, stitch from the center out, only as far as it does lie flat. Cut strips as directed, cutting only as many as possible before you need to realign and stitch more of the tube. Each time you cut a new series of strips, first cut a new straight edge on the tube.

5. Lay out the "rings" in the following order:
   AA BBB CCCCCC BB AAA BB CCCCC BB
6. Referring to the diagram, open each "ring" at the correct location to create the strip layout by tugging gently at each end of the seam to loosen the stitches. In the illustration at right, the black "squares" are the accent color.

Rhapsody Bargello

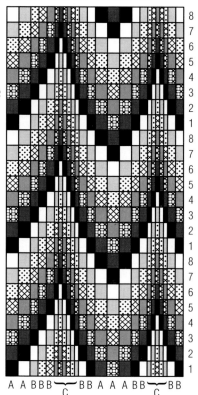

A A BBB ⌒C BB A A A BB ⌒C BB

♪ **NOTE:** Cut the remaining fabric into 1¼"-wide strips ("rings"). Then open and add them if necessary after making and positioning Spiral Bias (page 49).

7. Sew the strips together, using *scant* ¼"-wide seam allowances. It is not necessary to pin the strips together; just hold them together while you sew, matching each seam line by pulling gently or releasing the fabric strips. (Remember, this is recreational sewing. If seams don't match perfectly, it doesn't matter!)
8. Lay the jacket foundation on a flat surface. Center the completed Rhapsody Bargello on the jacket back at the neckline as shown in the jacket layout photo on page 46. Pin in place. Trim edges even with the foundation and stitch ¼" from raw edges.

✓ Prissy Puffing

MATERIALS

¼ yd. fabric

DIRECTIONS

1. Cut 4 strips, each 2" wide, across the fabric width.
2. Attach the gathering foot to your sewing machine and set the machine for the longest stitch length and the tightest tension. Test the stitch on a strip of fabric. The stitching should reduce the length of the strip by ⅓. If these settings create gathers that are too tight, reduce the tension and then the stitch length until the desired results are achieved.
3. Gather both long edges of each of the 4 strips so they match the length of the Rhapsody Bargello on the jacket back.

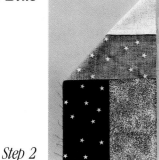

4. Pin a strip of Prissy Puffing next to long sides of Rhapsody Bargello. You may extend it to the bottom band as shown in the photo on page 46 if desired. Set aside the remaining strips to use on the sleeves and left jacket front.

♪ **NOTE:** If you do not have a gathering foot, set your machine for the longest stitch length and tightest tension. Stitch ⅛" from each raw edge of each strip. On some machines, this causes the fabric to gather on its own. If it doesn't on yours, pull up on the bobbin thread on each side of the strip.

✓ Spiral Bias

MATERIALS

⅛ yd. each of 2 different fabrics

DIRECTIONS *(See photos, below.)*

1. From each fabric, cut 1 strip, 4½" wide, across the fabric width. With the strips right sides together, stitch ¼" from one long edge. Press the seam toward the darker of the two fabrics.
2. Place the pieced strip on the table, right side up, and make a true bias (45° angle) fold. Carefully mark point "A" ¼" from both raw edges at the bottom right corner of the top layer of fabric.
3. Position the folded strip on the sewing machine and insert the needle in point A. Do not lower the presser foot yet.
4. Without moving the lower layer of fabric, align the bottom edge of the top layer of fabric with the raw edge of the lower layer and lower the presser foot. Stitch, even though it appears to be wrong! Continue lining up the raw edges and stitch to the lower edge. The result is an all-bias tube with the seam at a 45° angle from each folded edge.
5. Press the spiraled tube flat to crease the edges. Cut along both creased edges to create 2 strips.
6. Position one strip of Spiral Bias on each side of the Prissy Puffing on the jacket back foundation and pin in place. Trim so each strip is even with the outside edge and the Rhapsody Bargello. Stitch outer edges to the jacket foundation.

Spiral Bias

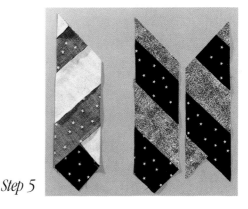

Step 2   *Step 4*   *Step 5*

✓ *Zigzag Strata*

MATERIALS

Seven 2"-wide strips of fabric

DIRECTIONS

1. Alternating the colors from dark to light to dark, sew the strips together in a band. Press all seams in one direction.

2. Fold the strip-pieced unit in half, wrong sides together. Place a ruler with the 45° line parallel to one of the seams and close to the folded edge. Cutting at a 45° angle, cut 4 strips, each 2" wide. You will have a total of 8 strips, 4 angling to the right and 4 to the left. Set aside pieces A and B for steps 6 and 7.

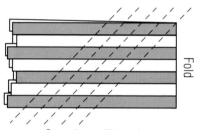

Cut strips at 45° angle.

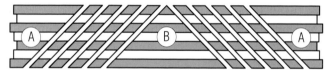

Right-pointing strips   Left-pointing strips

3. Unstack each set of strips and arrange pairs next to each other to create a zigzag pattern.

Arrange pairs next to each other.

4. Matching seams at intersections, sew these rows together and press seams in one direction. Using a rotary cutter, trim so top and bottom edges are straight. Or, you may choose to leave the zigzag points at one edge to overlap and appliqué to Quilting Crumbs. If so, do not use Prissy Puffing between Zigzag Strata and Quilting Crumbs.

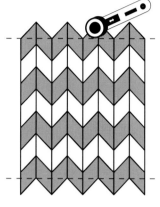

Trim away points.

5. Pin the completed Zigzag Strata to the upper left front of the jacket foundation. Pin a row of Prissy Puffing below the Zigzag Strata as shown in the jacket layout photo on page 46.

6. Sew the corner A triangles (left over from the strip-pieced unit) together with right sides facing and trim uneven edges. Press seam to one side. The resulting piece will be either a square or a rectangle, depending on the size and shape of "A." Set aside finished piece for step 5, page 52.

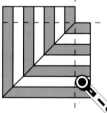

7. Use the remaining strip-pieced B triangle on the jacket lower back. Position it below the Rhapsody Bargello, removing 1 or 2 strips at the point to create a pieced trapezoid as shown in the jacket layout photo. Pin. Fill in the uncovered foundation space to the right and left of the triangle with any leftover fabric of your choice.

8. Cut a 1"- to 2"-wide strip of fabric for the lower edge of the jacket fronts and back and pin in place. You can use any fabric you like for this strip, but I like to use the same fabric that I use for the front band.

✓ *Flying Geese*

I learned this speedy method for making Flying Geese from Betty Gall of Quilter's Rule. She calls it "Cut-No-Triangles Flying Geese."

MATERIALS

¼ yd. fabric for main triangles
¼ yd. fabric for background triangles

DIRECTIONS

1. Cut a 5¼"-wide strip from the fabric for the main triangles. Cut the strip across the fabric width. Cut 4 squares, each 5¼" x 5¼", from the strip.

2. Cut 2 strips, each 2⅞" wide, from the fabric for the background triangles. From these strips, cut 16 background squares, each 2⅞" x 2⅞".

3. On the wrong side of the background squares, draw a diagonal line from one corner to the opposite one.

4. Stack squares in groups of 5 or 6 with the marked lines all in the same direction. Cut off a ½" triangle tip on one end as shown.

♪ **NOTE:** Be sure to make this cut across one of the corners that is intersected by a diagonal line.

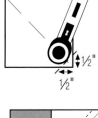

5. Position 2 small squares on top of 1 large square as shown, with right sides together and the cutoff corners toward the center. Machine stitch ¼" away from the marked line on both sides.

Stitch on both sides of marked line.

♪ **NOTE:** To chain piece, stitch on one side of the line on all 4 squares, then lift the presser foot, and without cutting the threads, turn the pieces and stitch down the second side on all 4 squares. This saves time and thread.

6. Cut on the marked line.

Cut apart.

7. Press the resulting small background triangles away from the main triangle in each unit.

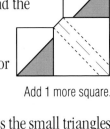

Press small triangles out.

8. Now place 1 small square on each of these units with right sides together and the cutoff corner toward the center seam line. Stitch ¼" away from the marked line on both sides. For quick chain piecing, do one side at a time on all pieces.

Add 1 more square.

9. Cut on the marked lines and press the small triangles away from the background triangle. This yields 2 Flying Geese units per unit for a total of 16.

Cut apart and press.

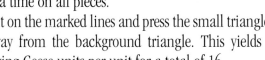

10. With right sides together, stitch the Flying Geese together in 2 rows of 8 units each as shown, using ¼"-wide seams. As you stitch, be careful not to stitch across the tips of the large triangles.

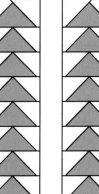

11. Sew the bottom ends of the two strips together and add a 1"- to 2"-wide border strip cut from a fabric of your choice to both long edges..

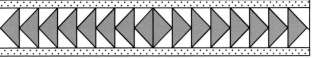

If you prefer, you may sew the strips together so the "geese" are all flying in the same direction.

12. Pin the completed Flying Geese unit to the right front of the jacket foundation as shown in the jacket layout photo on page 46.

✓Elinor's Fan

Elinor Peace Bailey, the "doll lady," devised this unusual strip-pieced fan.

MATERIALS

13" x 20" piece of muslin for foundation
Assorted strips of fabric, cut no wider than 2"

DIRECTIONS

1. Starting in one corner of the muslin foundation, pin a strip of fabric along the shorter edge, with the right side facing up as shown in the diagram. Point A is home point. Each strip of fabric you add to create Elinor's Fan must be stitched from this point to the next one (alphabetical order).

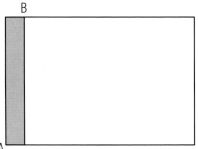

2. Lay the next strip, right side down, positioning it from Point A to Point B. Stitch ¼" from the raw edge of the second strip and trim the first strip even with the raw edge of the second. Finger press second strip to the right and pin in place. Trim excess even with the muslin foundation.

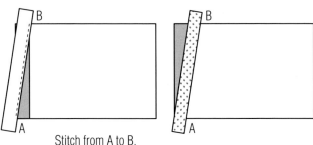

Stitch from A to B.

3. Position the third strip, right side down, from Point A to Point C. Stitch, trim, press, and pin as described for second strip.

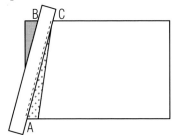

4. Repeat this process until the entire muslin piece is covered with strips of varying widths. Try to keep the muslin foundation free of wrinkles as you stitch. If small wrinkles do develop, don't worry, but make sure that the strip-pieced fan remains as flat as possible.

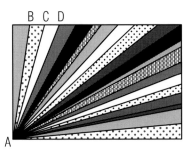

5. Position Elinor's Fan on the right jacket front next to the Flying Geese, with the top edge at the shoulder line as shown in the jacket layout photo on page 46. Place the piece made from the Zigzag Strata leftovers (step 6, page 50) on the sleeve next to the fan as shown in the jacket layout photo on page 46 and trim even with the fan piece. Trim Elinor's Fan even with the outer edge of the jacket foundation. Use the cutaway piece to cover the remainder of the foundation to the left of the Flying Geese and down to the bottom band already pinned in position (step 8, page 50). If you do not have enough leftover fan, strip piece to cover the remainder of the foundation. Stitch ¼" from the raw edges.

✓*Quilting Crumbs*

MATERIALS

⅓ yd. background fabric
⅓ yd. Wonder-Under or ⅓ yd. Fine Fuse (and Teflon press cloth)
⅓ yd. tulle netting in a dark color
Snips, strips, and threads left over from other patchwork pieces

DIRECTIONS

1. From the background fabric, the tulle, and the fusible web, cut rectangles large enough to cover the exposed jacket foundation below the Zigzag Strata and the Prissy Puffing and above the strip at the bottom edge. Apply fusible web to the *right* side of the background fabric rectangle. If you are using Wonder-Under, carefully remove the release paper and set aside to use in step 4.
2. To embellish the background rectangle with "crumbs," lay it right side up on a flat surface and randomly scatter fabric snippets and threads left over from this project over its surface.
3. Place the tulle on top of the crumbs and the foundation fabric.
4. If you are using Wonder-Under, place the release paper on top of the fabric layers. If you are using Fine Fuse, place the Teflon press cloth on top. Fuse the layers together, following the manufacturer's directions.
5. Pin the completed Quilting Crumbs to the left front as shown in the jacket layout photo on page 46. Trim edges even along side seam and where the piece meets the bottom band already in position. Machine stitch ¼" from the outer raw edges.

✓*Striking Stripes*

MATERIALS

⅓ yd. each of 2 different striped fabrics (A and B)

DIRECTIONS

1. Cutting across the fabric width, cut 2 strips, each 3" wide, and 1 strip, 1½" wide, from each striped fabric.
2. Sew the strips together to create 2 strip-pieced units as shown. Press seams away from the center strip in each unit.

3. Use a Quilter's Rule Jr. or other 4½" square cutting template to cut the strip-pieced units into 4½" squares as shown. You will get 5–7 squares from each unit (10–14 total).

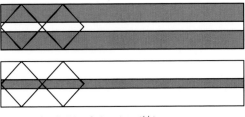

Cut Striking Stripes into 4½" squares.

4. Use the squares to create 2 or 3 design rows for the left sleeve foundation. When pleased with the arrangement, piece the rows together and press. Pin the completed piece to the sleeve foundation and use the triangles left over from cutting the squares to fill in and cover the foundation. Add a strip of Prissy Puffing above it and/or below the Striking Stripes as fill-in. Trim the Striking Stripes even with the edges of the foundation and stitch ¼" from the raw edges.

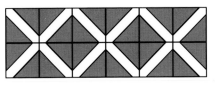

✓Flat Biscuits

MATERIALS

⅛ yd. muslin or other plain fabric
Twelve 4" squares of 2 to 6 different fabrics left over from
other patchwork pieces

DIRECTIONS

1. Cut twelve 3" biscuit backing squares from muslin. Pin the corners of a 4" biscuit square to the corners of a 3" backing square. The top square will be too large for the bottom square, so make a pleat in it at the center of each edge and pin in place. On the right side of the square, the folded edge of all pleats should point in a clockwise direction around the square.

2. Stitch around the pinned squares ⅛" from the raw edges. Then press each square to flatten out the excess fabric in the top square.

3. Stitch squares together in 2 rows of 6 biscuits each.

4. Pin the Flat Biscuits to the right sleeve foundation above the fabric at the bottom edge as shown in the jacket layout photo on page 46. Stitch ¼" from the raw edges of the sleeve and *then* trim biscuits even with the edges of the foundation. Add a row of Prissy Puffing above the biscuits, if necessary, to cover the remainder of the sleeve foundation.

✓Rose Petal Trim

MATERIALS

¼ yd. fabric

DIRECTIONS

1. Cut 1½"-wide, true bias strips from the fabric and join to make a continuous strip that measures 1½" x 50". Fold the continuous bias strip in half lengthwise, wrong sides together, but do not press.

2. Attach the gathering foot to your machine and set the stitch as described for Prissy Puffing in step 2 on page 49. Gather the strip, stitching ¼" from the raw edges.

3. Set aside gathered strip; add to the jacket during the finishing (page 56).

✓ Finishing the Foundation

1. Finish all raw edges on the jacket and sleeves with your choice of gimp, braid, or bias binding as shown on page 15.
2. Complete steps 8 and 9 on page 15.
3. With right sides together, stitch the continuous underarm seam of the jacket and sleeve as shown on page 15. Press the seam open.

✓ Neck/Front Band

1. Apply interfacing to the wrong side of each of the 3½"-wide neck/front band strips, following the manufacturer's directions for fusing. (See step 2, page 46, for band cutting information.)
2. With right sides together, stitch the two 3½"-wide strips together at one short end. Press seam open.

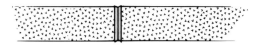

3. Fold the band in half lengthwise, wrong sides together, and press.
4. Pin the band to the jacket back neckline with right sides together, raw edges even, and the seam in the band at the center back. Continue pinning band to jacket front and trim excess band at each end even with the bottom edge of the jacket.

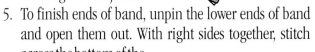

5. To finish ends of band, unpin the lower ends of band and open them out. With right sides together, stitch across the bottom of the band ½" from the raw edge.

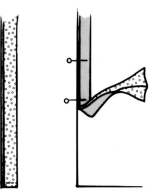

Trim the seam to ¼", clip the corner, and turn the band right side out again. Repin to the jacket, then stitch the band in place around the neckline and down the front edges.

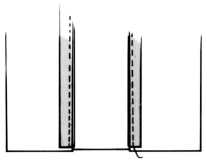

✓ Lining

1. Press under ¼" at the bottom edge of each sleeve in the jacket lining.
2. With right sides together, stitch the lining to the jacket ½" from the raw edges, leaving an 8"-long opening at the bottom edge of the center back for turning. Trim the seam to ¼". Turn right side out, pushing the lining sleeves into the jacket sleeves. Press.

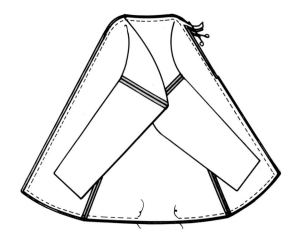

3. Turn in the seam allowances at the opening left for turning at the bottom edge of the jacket. Slipstitch the opening closed.

4. Add the Rose Petal Trim to the bottom of each sleeve in the following manner:

   a. Keeping the sleeve lining free, pin the Rose Petal Trim to the right side of each sleeve at the bottom edge, with raw edges even. Trim the strip to fit the sleeve circumference, allowing ¼"-wide seam allowances for joining the ends.

   b. Open out the folded trim at the cut ends and stitch, right sides together, using a ¼"-wide seam allowance. You may need to undo a few of the gathering stitches at each end in order to do this. Refold the trim and pin in place.

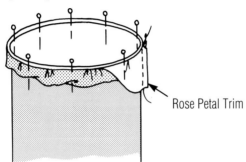

Rose Petal Trim

   c. Stitch trim to sleeve ¼" from the raw edge. Turn sleeve wrong side out.

   d. Turn the seam toward the sleeve and pin the bottom edge of the sleeve lining in place over the trim.

Do not catch lining in stitching.

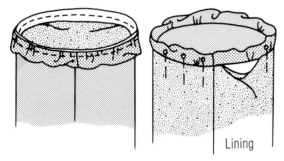

Lining

   e. Thread a needle with thread to match the Rose Petal fabric and knot. Hide the knot in the folded edge of the sleeve lining, then bring the thread through the lining and the Rose Petal Trim to the edge of the jacket sleeve. Take 3 stitches over the shirred ruffle and back through the jacket and the lining sleeves,

pulling the thread tight with each stitch to create a "petal." Bring thread through on the lining side after the third stitch.

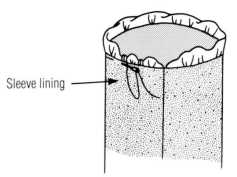

Sleeve lining

   f. Slip the needle and thread through the folded edge of the lining, taking 2–3 hemming stitches for ½", bring the needle through the fold, and make the next "petal" as described in step e. Continue until all the petals are complete and the lining sleeve is attached to the jacket sleeve.

5. With the jacket right side out, turn up a cuff of the desired width.

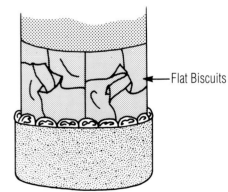

Flat Biscuits

6. Tack shoulder pads in place on inside of jacket.

Jacket Three by Maxine Gates, Victoria, Texas. Vertical placement of design elements and a solid-colored front band create a slimming illusion in this variation of Jacket Three. Maxine added a pocket (not included in the pattern) and placed Zigzag Strata on the diagonal to create her unique interpretation of Judy's original design.

Dark-to-light shading creates a classic Bargello inset. Alternating bands of dark prints in Spiral Bias create a showcase for the centerpiece. Cuffs finished with Rose Petal edging may be folded back, showing the contrasting lining.

Fluted Fantasia

▲ **Fragmented Bargello**　　　▲ **Spiraled Diamonds**

▲ **Fluted Fan**　　　　　　　　▲ **Stitched Slivers**

▲ **Tucked Cones**　　　　　　　▲ **Chevron Stripes**

1. Cut and prepare the jacket foundation and lining, following steps 1–3 on page 14.
2. Using the collar pattern for Jacket Four, cut 2 collars from the collar fabric and 1 from the interfacing.
3. Apply interfacing to the wrong side of 1 collar, following the manufacturer's directions. Set aside collar.

4. Make the patchwork pieces and apply to the jacket foundation, following the directions on pages 62–66.
5. Finish the jacket foundation, following the directions on page 67.
6. Following the directions on page 15, apply the interfacing (step 8) and then complete step 9.
7. Finish the jacket as directed on pages 67 and 68.

Interfacing

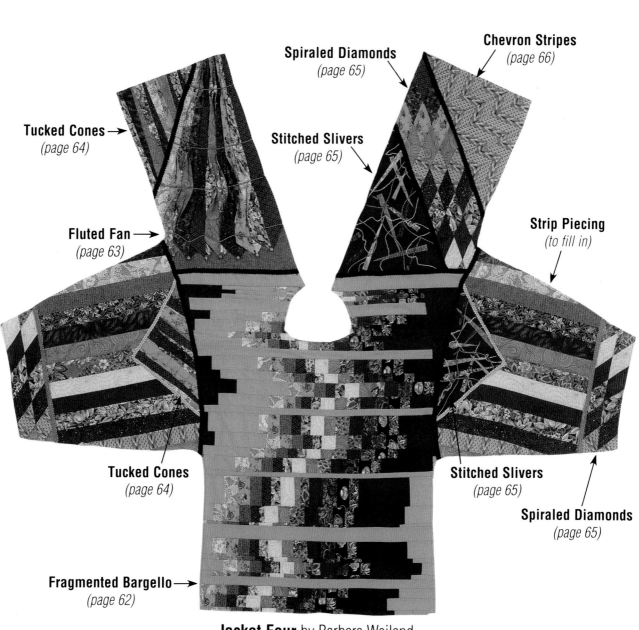

Spiraled Diamonds
(page 65)

Chevron Stripes
(page 66)

Tucked Cones →
(page 64)

Stitched Slivers
(page 65)

Fluted Fan →
(page 63)

Strip Piecing
(to fill in)

Tucked Cones
(page 64)

Stitched Slivers
(page 65)

Spiraled Diamonds
(page 65)

Fragmented Bargello →
(page 62)

Jacket Four by Barbara Weiland
Not Shown: Collar (page 65)

Shopping List

All yardage requirements listed are based on 44"-wide fabrics, unless otherwise noted. When using the same fabric in more than one patchwork piece, combine yardage requirements.

Jacket Foundation	2½ to 3 yds. cotton flannel or muslin
Jacket Lining	2½ to 3 yds. silky lining fabric
Interfacing	⅜ yd. lightweight fusible interfacing
Shoulder pads	Covered, raglan-style pads in the thickness of your choice
Fragmented Bargello	⅓ yd. solid-colored fabric (Contrast A)
	⅓ yd. solid-colored fabric (Contrast B)
	⅛ yd. each of 12 additional coordinating prints
Fluted Fan	⅛ yd. each of 8 different fabrics*
	3 yds. CrossLocked™ beads (Some will also be used for the Stitched Slivers.)
Tucked Cones	Leftovers from Fluted Fans
Spiraled Diamonds	⅛ yd. each of 10 different fabrics**
Stitched Slivers	½ yd. fabric for background
	10" square of Fine Fuse or other lightweight fusible web (and a Teflon press cloth)
	Decorative threads, such as metallic or cloisonné crochet thread or metallic ribbon
	Slivers saved from making Tucked Cones
Chevron Stripes	⅓ yd. of an *evenly* striped fabric
Collar and Facings	½ yd. fabric
Decorative Trim	Approximately 8 yds. (½" to ⅝" wide)
Notions	1½ yds. 1"-wide elastic
	2 frogs or 6 buttons for front closure

 * Choose 4 light and 4 dark fabrics, or choose 4 fabrics of one color and 4 of another, such as red and black. Or, choose 4 prints and 4 coordinating solids.

** Fabrics should contrast.

In addition to the fabrics and notions listed, you will need the following special supplies:
Cording or Beading Foot (An adjustable zipper foot can be substituted on some machines, but the beading foot is recommended for easier stitching and better results.)
Tucking Foot, if available for your machine
Twin needles to fit your machine (Consult your machine manual.)
9° Circle Wedge Ruler

FABRIC SELECTION TIPS

- A total of 14 different fabrics is required for this jacket.
- Since it is usually more difficult to find a striped fabric for Chevron Stripes after you've chosen all the other fabrics, find this fabric *first*.
- In addition to contrast fabrics A and B for the Fragmented Bargello, you will need 12 coordinating prints. You can include the striped fabric as one of these twelve. *Be sure to use strips of contrast A and B in one or more of the patchwork pieces for the front, so colors flow from front to back for design continuity.*

✓*Fragmented Bargello*

MATERIALS

⅓ yd. solid-colored fabric (Contrast A)
⅓ yd. solid-colored fabric (Contrast B)
⅛ yd. each of 12 additional coordinating printed fabrics

DIRECTIONS

1. Cut 1 strip, 6" wide, from Contrast A and 1 from Contrast B, cutting across the fabric width. Cut 1 strip from each of the 12 additional fabrics, varying the strip widths from 1½" to 3".
2. Sew the 12 strips together, using ¼"-wide seam allowances. Add Contrast A and Contrast B strips to opposite ends of the strip-pieced unit. Press all seams in one direction. When complete, the finished piece of 14 strips should measure at least 30" x 42".

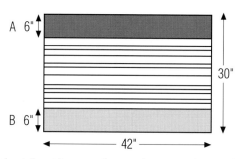

3. With right sides together and using a ¼"-wide seam, sew Contrast A to Contrast B to form a tube. Trim away the selvage on one end of the tube. Then cut the tube into strips ("rings"), varying the widths from ¾" to 3" wide.

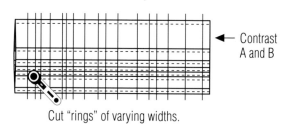

← Contrast A and B

Cut "rings" of varying widths.

♪ **NOTE:** The strip-pieced tube should lie flat when folded in half in preparation for stitching. If it does not, stitch from the center out, only as far as it does lie flat. Cut strips from the stitched section of the tube as directed above. Cut only as many as possible until you need to realign the raw edges and stitch more of the tube. Before cutting each new series of strips, first cut a new straight edge on the tube.

4. Open the "rings" into strips by cutting them with a scissors, one at a time, *through the A or B fabric only,* so that the contrast strips are always on one or both ends of each strip. Cut them so that the design forms an up-and-down stair-step arrangement as shown.

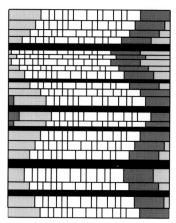

5. When all rings are cut apart and placed, cut a total of 6 strips from Contrast A and/or B fabric, varying the widths from ¾" to 2" wide. Place these between the pieced strips in a pleasing arrangement.
6. To make it easy to sew the strips together into a single piece, stack them in order to take to the sewing machine. Sew the strips together, using ¼"-wide seams. It is not necessary to try to match seam lines from row to row. Just pin the strips together at the top and bottom of each strip and sew. Press all seams in one direction.
7. Place on jacket back foundation with the contrast strips parallel to the bottom edge as shown in the jacket layout photo on page 60. The finished piece should be large enough to come up over the shoulder and pass the neckline edge at the center front by at least 1". If not, strip piece an additional strip or strips to the foundation.

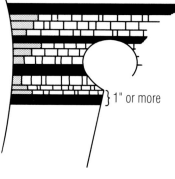

} 1" or more

✓ *Fluted Fan*

MATERIALS

⅛ yd. each of 8 different fabrics*
3 yds. CrossLocked beads

*Choose 4 light and 4 dark fabrics, or choose 4 fabrics of one
color and 4 of another, such as red and black. Or, choose 4
prints and 4 coordinating solids. One set will be Group 1 and
the other Group 2.*

DIRECTIONS

1. From each of the 8 fabrics, cut 1 strip, 2½" wide, cutting
   across the fabric width (crosswise grain).
2. With right sides together, sew a strip from Group 1 to
   a strip from Group 2, stitching ¼" from the raw edges.
   Do not press. Repeat with the remaining strips. You
   should have 4 sets of 2 strips each.

3. Work with one set of strips at a time. With the strips still
   facing each other in the sewing position, fold the strip
   in half crosswise. Cut 2 wedge sets from the folded strip,
   using the 9° Circle Wedge Ruler. Position the ruler with
   the center line *exactly* on the stitching line, making
   sure that the large end of the ruler is completely on the
   fabric. Don't worry if the narrow end extends beyond
   the fabric fold. Cut along the edge of the ruler.

Center line on ruler
Fold

Cut 2 wedge sets from joined strips.

   Cut the resulting piece (A) apart on the fold for 2 wedge
   sets. Cut the remaining piece (B) on the fold and save
   for the Tucked Cones and Stitched Slivers. Repeat with
   remaining strips.

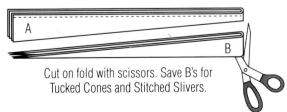

Cut on fold with scissors. Save B's for
Tucked Cones and Stitched Slivers.

4. With the wedges still
   folded right sides together,
   stitch across the wider end
   ¼" from the raw edges.
   Clip corners. Finger press
   seam to one side. Turn
   right side out and press
   with iron. It will look like the point of a man's tie.

5. Arrange wedges in a fan by placing 1 wedge on a flat
   surface so whole piece shows. Add next 7 wedge sets,
   always placing
   the first half of
   each one behind
   the previous
   wedge. This will
   give you an idea
   of how the piece
   will look when
   finished; you will
   sew wedges
   together and
   then pleat to
   create the
   "fluted" effect.

6. With raw edges even and right sides together, stitch all
   wedges together to make one big fan. Press all seams
   in one direction.
7. Place fan on a flat
   surface. Starting with
   the second set of wedges,
   fold the first wedge in
   each set in half down
   the center and press. The
   entire point of each
   wedge set should still
   show when the pleating
   is completed. Pin. Stitch
   folds in place across the
   small end of the fan.
8. Pin the Fluted Fan to the left front foundation as shown
   in the jacket layout photo on page 60. Stitch ¼" from
   front and bottom edges. Trim fan even with foundation
   at underarm. Place a fabric strip behind the fan points
   to cover foundation up to the edge of the Fragmented
   Bargello. Hand or machine tack fan points to the

background fabric. You may stitch 1" below the fan points to hold them in place and add CrossLocked beads as shown in step 9, following, and in the jacket layout photo.

9. A few inches from the bottom of the fan, open the fold of each wedge to reveal the inside pair and pin in place. Then stitch CrossLocked beads on top, using an adjustable zipper foot or a cording/beading foot that has one large groove on the bottom. To test the cording foot, place it on top of the beads on a flat surface. If you can easily and smoothly pull the beads through the groove in the bottom of the foot, it will work on the machine.

To use either type of foot, set the machine for a zigzag stitch that is wide enough to stitch over the beads without hitting them. To begin to stitch, turn the hand wheel manually to make sure the stitch is wide enough. Place the beads in position on the jacket and stitch over them. If you use the cording foot, the beads will lie under the foot; if you use the zipper foot, adjust so the beads lie next to the foot.

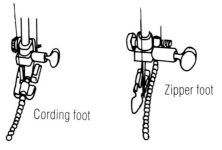

Cording foot

Zipper foot

10. A few inches above the beads, turn the fans back in the original direction and stitch across them, adding CrossLocked beads as before. A few inches higher up, flip the wedges as you did at the bottom and add CrossLocked beads as you stitch them in place. You may add buttons or beads to the fan points.

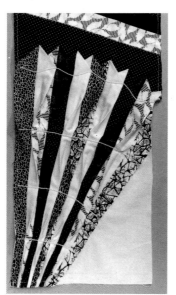

✓*Tucked Cones*

MATERIALS

Leftovers from Fluted Fans*

* You should have 4 stacks of cone pieces (2 of each fabric) left from each strip-pieced unit made for the Fluted Fans. This makes a total of 16 cones.

Leftover "cones"

DIRECTIONS

1. Cut the cones so they are 14" long, trimming slivers away as shown. Set slivers aside to use for Stitched Slivers, page 65.

sliver   14" cone

2. Arrange the cones, alternating the fabric colors and the broad and narrow ends. Sew the cones together into one continuous piece, using ¼"-wide seam allowances. Press all seams in one direction.

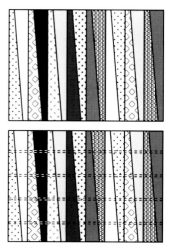

3. Insert a twin needle in your machine and thread machine with 2 spools of thread. To help define the tucks, replace the regular presser foot with a tucking foot, if you have one for your machine.

4. Stitch across the cones, making several rows in a spacing that pleases you. *Do not press the tucks.*

5. Place the completed Tucked Cones on the left front below the Fluted Fans and trim even with the foundation. Pin in place and stitch ¼" from the underarm edge. Cut the remaining piece into a triangle, making it as large as possible. Position it at the top of the left sleeve with the center of the long edge at the shoulder mark. See jacket layout photo on page 60.

✓Spiraled Diamonds

MATERIALS

⅛ yd. each of 10 different fabrics

DIRECTIONS

1. From each of the 10 fabrics, cut 1 strip 2¼" wide, cutting across the fabric width.
2. Sew the strips together, using ¼"-wide seams and offsetting each new piece by 2" as shown. Press all seams in one direction. The finished piece should be approximately 18" wide.

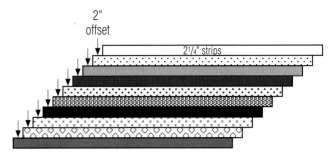

3. Align the 45° line on a rotary-cutting ruler at point A/B on the strip-pieced unit as shown and trim away the staggered edge. Then cut 7 strips, each 2¼" wide, cutting them parallel to the new cut edge. Set aside remaining strip-pieced fabric to use on the sleeves.

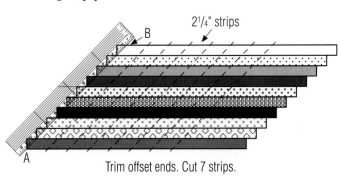

Trim offset ends. Cut 7 strips.

4. Arrange strips side by side in a consistent pattern as shown, above right. Sew the strips together in 1 set of 3 strips and 2 sets of 2 strips each, using ¼"-wide seam allowances.

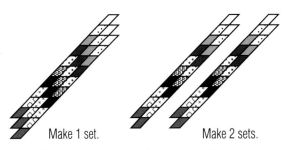

Make 1 set.   Make 2 sets.

5. Position a 2-strip set of Spiraled Diamonds at the bottom edge of each sleeve so the designs are mirror images of each other. Pin in place and trim even with the foundation. Stitch ¼" from raw edges.
6. Cut off the end of the 3-strip set of Spiraled Diamonds as shown.

Cut away the
3 bottom diamonds.

7. Pin the strip to the right jacket front, placing it diagonally as shown in the jacket layout photo on page 60. Trim even with the foundation edge and stitch ¼" from the underarm and front edges to secure.

✓Stitched Slivers

MATERIALS

½ yd. fabric (for background)
10" square of Fine Fuse or other lightweight fusible web (and a Teflon press cloth)
Decorative threads, such as metallic or cloisonné threads or metallic ribbon
Slivers saved from making Tucked Cones
CrossLocked beads

DIRECTIONS

1. Cut an 18" square from the background fabric.
2. Place the Teflon press cloth on the ironing board with the piece of Fine Fuse on top. Then place the Tucked

Cone slivers *right side up* on the Fine Fuse. Fold the Teflon press cloth so it covers the slivers and any excess Fine Fuse. Fuse, following manufacturer's directions. Use a rough sponge to remove any Fine Fuse that is stuck to the Teflon press cloth.

3. Cut the slivers apart and place randomly on the right side of the background square. Fuse them to the square, using the Teflon press cloth to protect the bottom of your iron from any Fine Fuse that might be exposed at the edge of the slivers.

4. Now the fun begins! Stitch over the slivers, adding your choice of decorative elements, including CrossLocked beads, metallic ribbons, and metallic threads. You can also use the twin needle and the tucking foot to stitch over the slivers for added interest.

5. Place the finished Stitched Slivers on the right front between the Spiraled Diamonds and the Fragmented Bargello as shown in the jacket layout photo on page 60. Trim to fit. Cut the remaining piece into a triangle and place at the top edge of the right sleeve, with the center of the piece at the shoulder marking. Pin. Stitch ¼" from raw edges of jacket foundation.

✓Chevron Stripes

MATERIALS

⅓ yd. of an evenly striped fabric

DIRECTIONS

1. With the fabric folded selvage to selvage, cut a 10"-wide strip across the fabric width.
2. Without unfolding the strip, cut the folded end at a 45° angle. Then cut 1 strip, 1" wide; 2 strips, each 2" wide; and 1 strip, 3" wide. Since you cut through 2 layers of fabric, you will have a total of 8 strips.

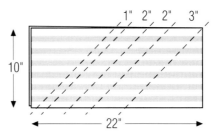

3. Lay out the strips in the width arrangement shown so the stripes form a chevron where the strip edges meet. Stitch together, using ¼"-wide seams.

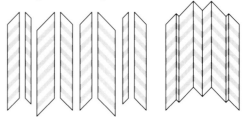

4. Position a point of the Chevron Stripes in the lower corner of the right jacket front as shown. Cut the top edge even with the bottom edge of Spiraled Diamonds. Trim the bottom and side even with the outer edges of the foundation and stitch ¼" from the raw edges to secure.
5. Using the corner pieces that remained after cutting strips from the striped fabric, cut pieces to continue the pattern to the left and right as needed, to cover the foundation where it is not covered by the Chevron Stripes.

✓Finishing the Foundation

1. Cover the exposed area of the foundation on each sleeve with strip piecing or a piece of fabric cut to fit. Use leftovers from the Spiraled Diamonds, if desired.
2. Finish all raw edges on the jacket and sleeve with your choice of gimp, braid, or bias binding as shown on page 15.
3. Stitch the sleeves to the jacket, press seams open, and cover the armhole seam with your choice of trim.
4. Apply interfacing to the jacket as shown in step 8 on page 15. Then complete step 9.
5. With right sides together, stitch the continuous underarm seam of the jacket and sleeve as shown on page 15 and press seams open. Repeat with the lining.

✓Finishing

1. Stitch the collars with right sides together, leaving the bottom edge open. Trim seams to ¼", clip curves, and trim across the corners to reduce bulk. Turn right side out and press. Set aside.

2. With wrong sides together, pin the lining to the jacket along all raw edges, including sleeve edges.
3. For the facings, cut 4 strips of fabric, each 3" wide, cutting across the fabric width. For bottom facing, stitch 2 strips together at the short ends. Press seam open. Press under ¼" on one long edge of each strip.

Facing strip

4. With right sides together, pin facing strip to the bottom edge of the jacket and stitch, using a ½"-wide seam allowance. Trim the seam to ¼".

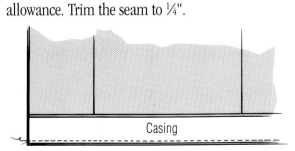

Casing

Turn facing to inside and press. Edgestitch along folded edge, beginning and ending at side seams and leaving front unstitched. Stitch again 1⅛" from the first row of stitching to form casings for 2 pieces of elastic.

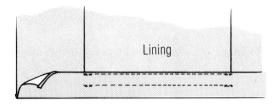

Lining

5. Cut 2 pieces of elastic that are 1" shorter than the measurement of the jacket back at the bottom edge from side seam to side seam. Thread the elastic through the casings and pin in place at the side seams. On the right side of the jacket, stitch "in the ditch" (next to the seam line) at both side seams to secure the elastic.

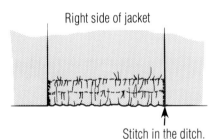

Right side of jacket

Stitch in the ditch.

6. Pin the casing edges in place on the jacket fronts and blindstitch close to the folded edge. Trim excess casing even with front edges of jacket.

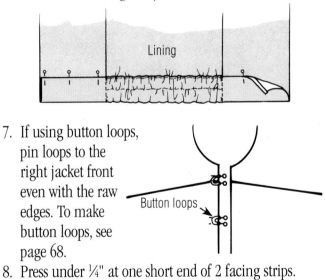

Lining

7. If using button loops, pin loops to the right jacket front even with the raw edges. To make button loops, see page 68.

Button loops

8. Press under ¼" at one short end of 2 facing strips.

9. With right sides together and raw edges even, pin a facing strip to the jacket along each front edge. Begin pinning at the bottom edge. There will be excess facing to be cut off at the neck edge. Stitch, using a ½"-wide seam allowance. Trim the facing seams to ¼". Turn facings to inside and press. Trim the excess facing strip even with the raw edge of the jacket neckline.

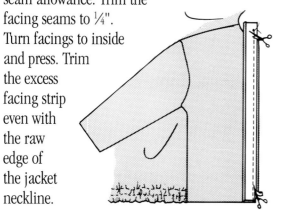

10. With right sides together, pin the collar to the neckline edge, leaving the lining and facings free. Stitch. Trim neckline seam to ¼" and turn toward the jacket. Press. Turn facings to inside and slipstitch in place. Turn under the lining and facing seam allowances along the neckline edge and slipstitch in place to cover the raw edges of the collar.

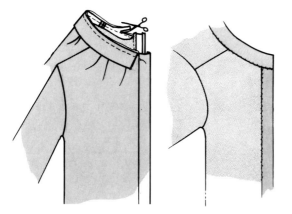

11. Cut the remaining facing strip in half and press under ¼" at one short end of each strip.

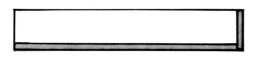

12. With right sides together, pin a facing strip to the bottom edge of each sleeve, lapping the raw end over the folded end. Trim away excess facing. Stitch ½" from the raw edge. Trim the seam to ¼"; turn and press.

Hand or machine stitch the folded edge of the facing in place; slipstitch the short ends together as shown.

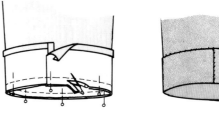

13. Sew buttons to the left jacket front opposite the loops or attach 1 or 2 frogs for the front closure.

14. Tack the shoulder pads in place on the inside of the jacket.

✓Button Loops

1. To make your own button loops, cut a strip of fabric 1¼" wide and long enough to accommodate the number of buttons you plan to use. For example, a strip 1¼" x 12½" should accommodate five ¾"-diameter buttons.

2. Fold the strip in half, right sides together, and place a piece of string, 1" longer than the strip, inside, next to the fold. Stitch across the short end ⅛" from the raw edge, catching the string in the stitches. Pivot and continue to stitch ⅛" from the long edge, being careful *not* to catch the string in the stitching.

3. Slide the strip back along the string to turn it right side out and cut off the string at the stitched short end.

4. Cut the strip into the lengths required for the buttons you are using.

Jacket Four by Maxine Gates, Victoria, Texas. Beading and decorative stitching add design emphasis to Stitched Slivers and Three-Dimensional Tucks. Maxine used only two colors plus silver accents to create this dramatic variation of Judy's original multi-colored jacket.

Values of red used with gradations of black in the Fragmented Bargello pattern create the effect of movement and refracted light on the jacket back.

Woven Roundelay

- Woven Bargello
- Modified Sashiko
- Three-Dimensional Tucks
- Stitch and Slash
- Knotted Tubes
- The Long and Short of It

1. Before you cut the foundation, it's important to note that the sleeves in this jacket are finished with bias binding and require no seam allowance at the bottom edge. To make sure that the sleeve will be the correct finished length before you add the patchwork pieces to the sleeve foundation, pin the jacket front, back, and sleeve pattern pieces together along the ½" seam lines and try on. Be sure to tuck the shoulder pad in place as it will raise the jacket on your shoulders and thereby shorten the sleeve. Adjust the sleeve length if needed, then cut the jacket pieces from the foundation.

This is also an excellent time to determine which of the two jacket lengths you prefer and to adjust the finished length, if required.

2. Cut and prepare the jacket foundation and lining, following steps 1–3 on page 14.

3. Make the patchwork pieces and prepare the bias binding, following the directions on pages 74–81.

4. Finish the jacket foundation, following the directions on page 82.

5. Following the directions on page 15, apply the interfacing (step 8), and complete step 9.

6. Complete the jacket as directed under "Finishing" on page 82.

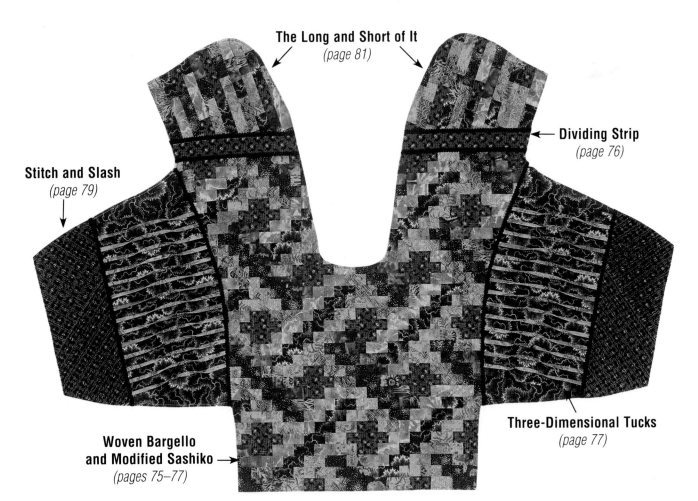

The Long and Short of It
(page 81)

Dividing Strip
(page 76)

Stitch and Slash
(page 79)

Three-Dimensional Tucks
(page 77)

Woven Bargello and Modified Sashiko →
(pages 75–77)

Jacket Five (short version) by Ursula Reikes
Not Shown: Edge Finish (pages 81–82)

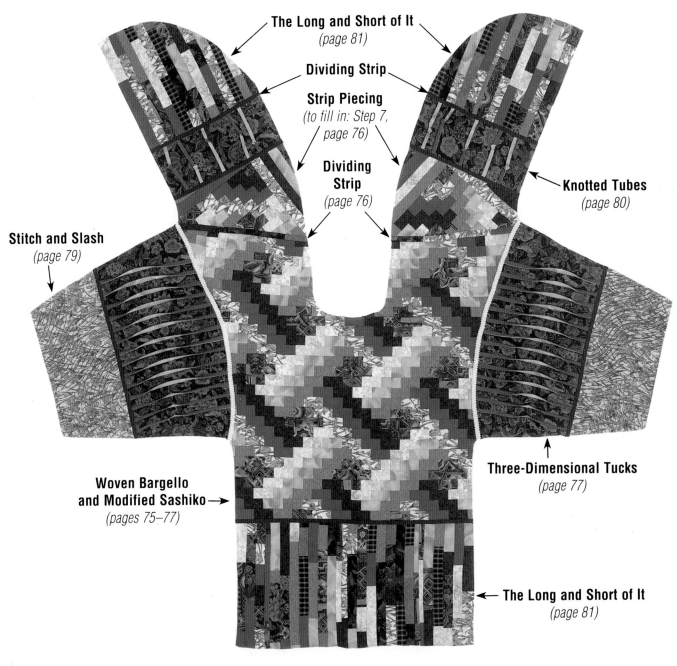

The Long and Short of It
(page 81)

Dividing Strip

Strip Piecing
(to fill in: Step 7, page 76)

Dividing Strip
(page 76)

Knotted Tubes
(page 80)

Stitch and Slash
(page 79)

Woven Bargello and Modified Sashiko →
(pages 75–77)

Three-Dimensional Tucks
(page 77)

The Long and Short of It
(page 81)

Jacket Five (long version) by Marta Estes
Not Shown: Edge Finish (pages 81–82)

FABRIC SELECTION TIPS

All yardage requirements listed are based on 44"-wide fabrics, unless otherwise noted. When using the same fabric in more than one patchwork piece, combine yardage requirements.

Jacket Foundation	2½ to 3 yds. cotton flannel or muslin
Jacket Lining	2½ to 3 yds. silky lining fabric
Interfacing	⅜ yd. lightweight, fusible interfacing
Shoulder Pads	Covered, raglan-style pads in the thickness of your choice
Woven Bargello	½ yd. each of fabrics A-1, A-2, and A-3 for Set 1*
	½ yd. each of fabrics B-1, B-2, and B-3 for Set 2*
	½ yd. of contrast fabric C
Modified Sashiko	Twin needles with large eyes (Schmetz 3,0/90 or 100)
	Buttonhole twist, metallic, or other decorative thread in a color that contrasts with fabric C
Three-Dimensional Tucks	1 yd. large-scale, uneven print for background
	½ yd. each of 2 fabrics (A and B) for the tucks
Stitch and Slash	¼ yd. each of 4 different fabrics
	Decorative thread in a coordinating color
Knotted Tubes	Leftovers from making 3-D Tucks
The Long and Short of It	Leftovers from cutting strips for Woven Bargello
Edge Finish	½ yd. fabric for bias binding around jacket and sleeve edges
Decorative Trim	Approximately 5 yds. (½" to ⅝" wide)
Frog Closure	

* Choose 2 sets of blending fabrics, such as gradations of purple and green.

- Choose a large, uneven print for the background of the Three-Dimensional Tucks. All remaining fabrics should coordinate with this fabric.

- First select two sets of three fabrics each, in two color families from the background print. For example, select three shades of green and three shades of purple.

- Next, select a fabric for the "cross" in the bargello. It should contrast with the bargello colors.

- Choose two fabrics that contrast with the large print for the Three-Dimensional Tucks.

- Use any four of the fabrics selected above for the Stitch and Slash.

- Choose fabric for binding the outer edges last. In most cases, the contrast for the bargello cross is a good choice for the binding.

✓Woven Bargello

This technique was developed by Jackie Robinson of Animas Quilts and is the subject of her booklet *Weaver Fever*. It is included here with her permission. For more information on *Weaver Fever*, contact Animas Quilts Publishing, 600 Main Ave., Durango, CO 81301 or call (303) 247-2582.

MATERIALS

½ yd. each of fabrics A-1, A-2, and A-3 for Set 1*
½ yd. each of fabrics B-1, B-2, and B-3 for Set 2*
½ yd. of contrast fabric C

* Choose 2 sets of blending fabrics, such as gradations of purple and green.

Cutting Chart

Fabric	No. of Strips	Strip Size	Fabric	No. of Strips	Strip Size
⊡ A-1	2	1½" x 16"	▨ B-2	7	2½" x 16"
	6	2½" x 16"	▩ B-3	7	2½" x 16"
⊠ A-2	2	1½" x 16"	▉ C	1	4½" x 16"
	6	2½" x 16"		1	3½" x 16"
▦ A-3	2	1½" x 16"		4	2½" x 16"
	6	2½" x 16"		1	1½" x 16"
▢ B-1	2	1½" x 16"			
	6	2½" x 16"			

Set remaining fabric aside for The Long and Short of It.

DIRECTIONS

1. Sew the strips together in the sets shown, using ¼"-wide seam allowances.

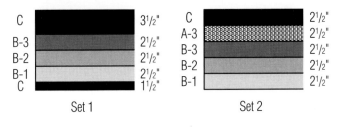

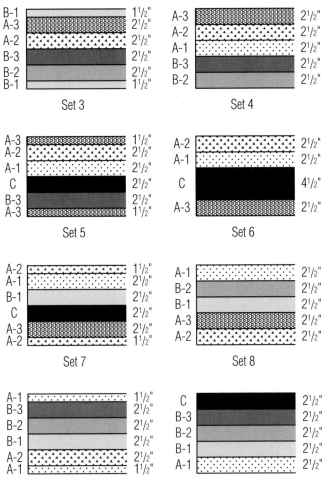

Each finished set should measure approximately 10½" x 16". Press all seams toward the first strip in each set. Pin or tape a tag that identifies the set by number to the first strip of each one.

2. Layer sets 1 to 5 together and 6 to 10 together. Using a rotary cutter and ruler, trim the short edge of the stack so it is straight and perpendicular to the long edge.

   Keeping the sets layered, make 9 cuts for the short jacket, or 10 cuts for the long one. Space the cuts 1½" apart.

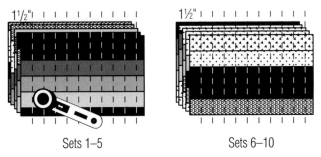

3. Divide the strips into 9 (or 10) stacks of 1½"-wide strips. Each stack should contain 1 strip from each set, lay-

ered in numerical order (10 strips per stack). From here on, the set numbers become row numbers.

4. Lay out the strips from one stack, placing them in numerical order. Stitch the strips together row by row, using ¼"-wide seam allowances. Seams will not match from row to row, but all seam allowances on each strip should be pressed in the same direction. Check for this before stitching one row to the next. Refer to the diagram for accuracy of placement. Repeat with the remaining stacks of strips. You should have a total of 9 (or 10) identical blocks.

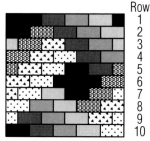

Row
1
2
3
4
5
6
7
8
9
10

Make 9 (or 10) identical blocks.

5. Arrange 9 of the blocks with 3 rows across and 3 rows down, placing Row 1 in each block at the top edge of each horizontal row. Set the tenth block aside to use in the longer jacket version.

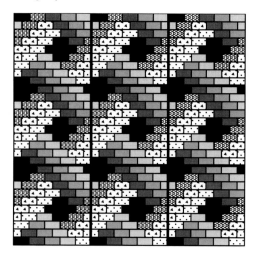

6. *For the short jacket:* Place the Woven Bargello piece at the bottom edge of the jacket back with raw edges even. It should extend over the shoulder to the front. Refer to the jacket layout photo on page 72. Pin in place and trim edges even with the foundation. Stitch ¼" from outer edges.

For the long jacket: Position the piece of Woven Bargello with the first seam line (between Rows 1 and 2) aligned with the shoulder seam lines on the jacket foundation at the armhole edges. Refer to the jacket layout photo on page 73. You will have 1 row of blocks on the front of the jacket and 2 on the back. Trim excess bargello even with foundation neckline and front edge.

Stitch ¼" from the raw edges.

On the longer jacket back, measure from the bottom of the bargello to the bottom edge. Measure up the same distance from the bottom edge of each jacket front and draw a line on the foundation. This marks the bottom edge for the Knotted Tubes (page 80).

Bargello

7. *For the long jacket only:* Cut the tenth Woven Bargello block in half on the diagonal as shown. Position one of the resulting triangles on each jacket front, placing the long edge of the triangle at the bottom edge of the Woven Bargello as shown below.

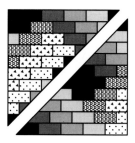

Draw a line on the foundation across each front just below the tips of the triangles. Cover the remaining foundation on each side of the triangle with strip piecing, ending the strips at the line you drew. See "Note" on pages 14–15 for strip-piecing directions.

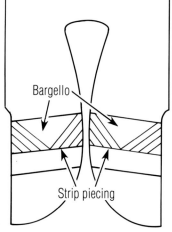

Bargello

Strip piecing

8. Do the Modified Sashiko stitching (page 77) now.

9. For either jacket version, cut 2 dividing strips, each 1½" to 2½" wide, and position below the Woven Bargello on the jacket fronts. If this does not reach to the point where The Long and Short of It will begin on the long jacket (page 81), cut and add more strips. If it goes beyond the drawn line, use narrower strips.

✓Modified Sashiko

MATERIALS

Twin needles with large eyes (Schmetz 3,0/90 or 100)
Buttonhole twist, metallic, or other decorative thread in
a color that contrasts with fabric C

DIRECTIONS

1. Replace the regular needle in your sewing machine
   with a twin needle. Thread the machine with 2 spools
   of the chosen decorative thread. Use regular sewing
   machine thread in the bobbin in a color that matches
   the "crosses" in the completed Woven Bargello.

2. Set the stitch length at 4 to 8 stitches per inch and test
   on a scrap of fabric. It may be necessary to loosen the
   tension when sewing with heavier decorative thread.

3. Stitch around each cross in the bargello, beginning on
   a side rather than in a corner. Stitch with the outside
   edge of the presser foot along the seam line all the way
   around the cross. If you want the stitches closer to the
   seam line, move the needle position to the right,
   making sure that it will still stitch without hitting the
   throat plate of the machine.

   As you approach a corner, raise the needles so
   you can pivot. When you insert the needles to continue stitching, insert them in the stitches closest to
   the seam line.

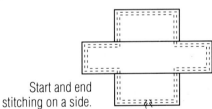

Start and end
stitching on a side.

   Be sure to leave tails of thread at the beginning and
end of the stitching. Pull them through to the wrong
side, tie them off close to the foundation, and trim the
excess threads.

✓Three-Dimensional Tucks

MATERIALS

1 yd. large-scale, uneven print for background
½ yd. each of 2 fabrics (A and B) for the tucks

DIRECTIONS

1. If you did not check the sleeve length as directed in step
   1 on page 72, do so now and adjust, if necessary.

2. The finished Stitch and Slash (page 79) will cover the
   lower 7" of the sleeve. To determine how wide to cut the
   background print for the tucks, subtract 7" from the
   actual length of the sleeve foundation. Cut 2 pieces of
   the background fabric the determined width, cutting
   from selvage to selvage.

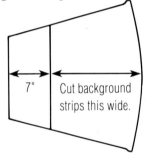

7"   Cut background
strips this wide.

3. Unfold the 2 pieces and layer the 2 pieces. Cutting both
   layers of fabric at the same time, cut 20 strips, each 1½"
   wide, cutting parallel to the selvage edge. Save the
   remaining uncut fabric. As you cut, separate the strips
   into 2 stacks of 20 strips each, *placing them face down
   and keeping the strips in order. This is important!*
   After you make the tucks, you will sew them between
   the strips in the same order the strips were cut so the
   original design in the fabric is still obvious even though
   it is broken by the tucks.

4. Cut 12 strips each from fabrics A and B for the tucks. Cut them ¾" wide from selvage to selvage.

5. With right sides together, sew each strip of A to a strip of B, stitching a scant ¼" from one long edge. Press the seam open or to one side.

6. Now fold the strips in half along the seam line with wrong sides together and press flat. Cut into tucking strips that measure the same length as the strips cut from your background print.

7. Make Three-Dimensional Tucks for one sleeve at a time. Turn each stack of strips cut from the background fabric right side up. The first strip you cut should be on top. Using 1 stack of background strips, place strip #1 right side up on your sewing machine. Place a tucking strip on top of it with raw edges even. Place the next background strip face down on the tuck. Stitch ³⁄₁₆" from the raw edges.

   Open out the second background strip and position a tucking strip on top with raw edges even. Make sure that the same color is on top in the tucking strip as in the first one. Place the third background strip face down on the tuck. Stitch a scant ³⁄₁₆" from the raw edges. Continue in this manner until you have a piece wide enough to cover the width of the sleeve where Stitch and Slash and Three-Dimensional Tucks meet. Press all tucks in one direction. Repeat this process for the second sleeve. Set aside the leftover tucking strips for Knotted Tubes (for long jacket only).

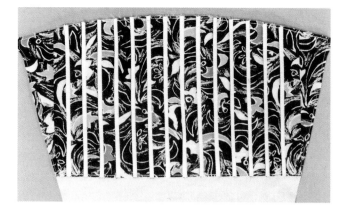

8. Stitch the Three-Dimensional Tucks to each sleeve foundation, stitching along the top and bottom edges of the tucks. Cover the exposed foundation on each side with a piece of the leftover background fabric. Pin a piece to each side of the tucks, with right sides together and raw edges even. Stitch ¼" from the raw edges through all layers, flip, and press flat. Trim even with outside edges of the sleeve and stitch ¼" from edge.

9. In the center of each sleeve, turn the tucks in the opposite direction from the way they are lying and press. Hand tack them in place from the wrong side of the foundation, or bar tack them from the front by hand or machine, using matching thread.

Step 5   *Step 7*

✓Stitch and Slash

MATERIALS

¼ yd. each of 4 different fabrics*
Decorative thread in a coordinating color

A strip of fabric will be left over from each of these 4 fabrics to use for dividing strips and/or for The Long and Short of It.

DIRECTIONS

1. Lay each fabric out flat and then layer them with the most dominant fabric on top, graduating to the least dominant one on the bottom. Cutting through all layers, cut a strip 7" wide. Then cut the stack of strips in half crosswise. Each 7"-wide piece will be approximately 21" long. Pin the layers together in each stack.

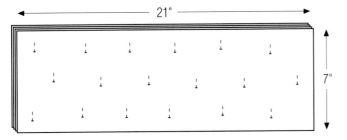

2. Stitch through all 4 layers of fabric, following a design on the top fabric or creating your own design. You may start stitching from any one of the four raw edges and stitch your design, ending at another raw edge. Space stitching lines approximately ¼" apart to create channels for cutting. *Do not stitch across any of the stitching lines.* Stitch up and down, round and round, and in and out to hold all layers together, always creating channels for cutting. The closer to bias grain your stitching runs, the less raveling you will get after cutting the channels and washing the piece.

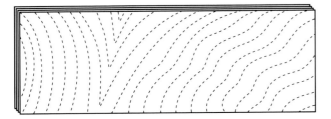

3. Using a small, sharp scissors and starting at a raw edge, cut through the top 3 layers of fabric in every stitching channel. Be careful not to cut through the bottom layer of fabric.

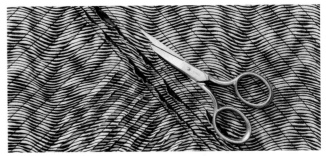

4. When slashing (cutting) is complete, wet the pieces *only if the fabrics you used were prewashed.* If the fabric has not been prewashed, wash it with detergent. Then put the wet pieces in a dryer with other items. When completely dry, remove them from the dryer and shake to remove loose threads. You may need to trim excess threads away.

5. Pin a piece of Stitch and Slash to the bottom edge of each sleeve foundation. Trim even with the edges of the sleeve and stitch ¼" from the raw edges.

✓ *Knotted Tubes* (for long jacket only)

MATERIALS

Leftover tucking strips from making Three-Dimensional Tucks
Leftover fabrics from other patchwork pieces

DIRECTIONS

1. Create tubes out of the leftover tucking strips by stitching them, right sides together, along the remaining long raw edges. Turn tubes right side out and press.

♪ **NOTE:** To make it easy to turn the tubes right side out, stitch with a cord inside as shown for Button Loops on page 68.

Original stitching

Leftover Tucking Strip

Stitch here
to form a tube.

2. To determine how wide to cut a strip of fabric to cover the foundation in the area between the dividing strip and The Long and Short of It, measure the jacket front from the line you drew to the bottom of the dividing strip. Cut 1 strip for each jacket front from a fabric left over from other patchwork pieces. Cut the finished tubes the same length plus ¾".

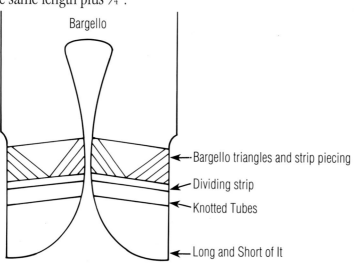

Bargello

Bargello triangles and strip piecing

Dividing strip

Knotted Tubes

Long and Short of It

3. Tie a knot in each tube, spacing the knots at different levels on the tubes. Tie some tubes so fabric A is the knot and fabric B is the strip showing above and below the knot. Tie others so fabric B is the knot and fabric A shows above and below the knot. Or, tie and position so that fabric A shows above the knot and B shows below the knot or vice versa.

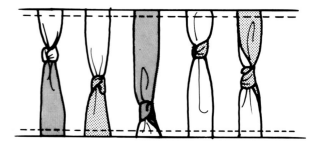

4. Pin knotted tubes to each fabric strip and stitch across the ends to hold the tubes in place on the background strip cut earlier. Trim tube excess even with strip edges. Pin completed Knotted Tubes to the jacket fronts as shown in the jacket layout photo on page 73.

✓ The Long and Short of It

MATERIALS

Leftovers from cutting strips for Woven Bargello

DIRECTIONS

1. Make a clean cut on each of the remaining bargello fabrics. Then cut the pieces into 1½"-wide strips of varying lengths.

2. If you are making the longer jacket, determine how long to make The Long and Short of It to fill in the back below the Woven Bargello and the fronts below the Knotted Tubes. If you are making the short version of the jacket, you will need only enough to cover the area on the fronts below the Woven Bargello and the dividing strip.

3. Stitch the 1½"-wide strips together, end to end, to make one long piece. Cut into a variety of lengths and then sew the new pieces together into one very long piece.

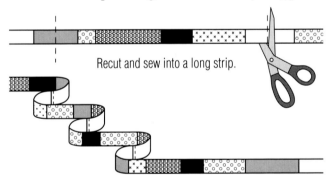

Recut and sew into a long strip.

4. Cut this strip into pieces the length determined in step 2. Position the strips on the jacket fronts and back in a pleasing arrangement, then sew them together, using ¼"-wide seam allowances.

5. Pin The Long and Short of It to the jacket foundation as shown in the jacket layout photos on pages 72 and 73. Trim even with foundation. Stitch ¼" from the outer edges.

✓ Bias Binding

MATERIALS

½ yd. fabric

DIRECTIONS

1. Open out the fabric and turn down one corner to form a triangle. Cut along the fold line.

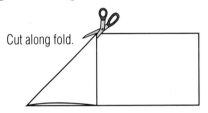

Cut along fold.

With right sides together, sew the cutaway triangle to the opposite end of the fabric, using a ¼"-wide seam allowance. Press seam open. Position ruler for a cut 3" from the diagonal edge. Before rotary cutting, make a 1"-long mark at each long edge. Then cut between the marks, leaving 1" uncut at each edge. Continue across the remainder of the piece, spacing cuts 3" apart and leaving 1" uncut at each edge.

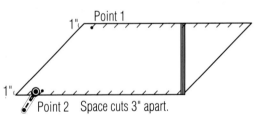

Point 1

1"

Point 2 Space cuts 3" apart.

2. Fold the strip in half lengthwise, right sides together, and match Point 1 to Point 2. Pin until you have formed a spiral cylinder of fabric. Stitch, using a ¼"-wide seam allowance.

3. Cut the cylinder open across the seam lines to form one continuous strip of bias binding. Press seams open.

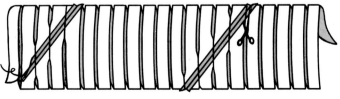

4. Fold binding strip in half, wrong sides together, and press, being careful not to stretch it.

✓ Finishing the Foundation

1. Finish all raw edges on the jacket and sleeves with your choice of gimp, braid, or bias binding as shown on page 15.
2. Stitch the sleeves to the jacket. Press the seams open and cover the armhole seam with your choice of trim.
3. Complete steps 8 and 9 on page 15.
4. With right sides together, stitch the continuous underarm seam of the jacket and sleeve as shown on page 15 and press the seam open. Repeat with the lining.

✓ Finishing

1. *With wrong sides together,* pin the lining to the jacket along all raw edges, including the sleeve edges.
2. Open out the binding and turn under one edge at a 45° angle as shown. Trim, leaving a ¼" allowance. Refold.

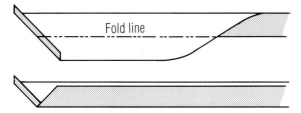

Fold line

3. With right sides together, pin the binding to the jacket neckline, front, and bottom edges, beginning and ending at the center back as shown. Stitch ¼" from the raw edges.

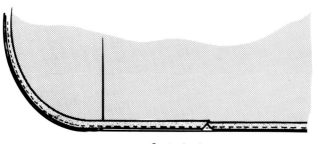

Center back

4. Turn the binding to the inside and slipstitch in place.

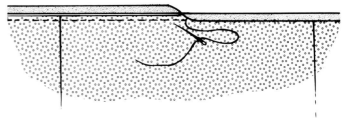

5. Bind the bottom edges of the sleeves in the same manner.
6. Attach a frog closure to the jacket fronts, positioning it at the edge of the dividing strip below the Woven Bargello.
7. Tack the shoulder pads in place on the inside of the jacket.

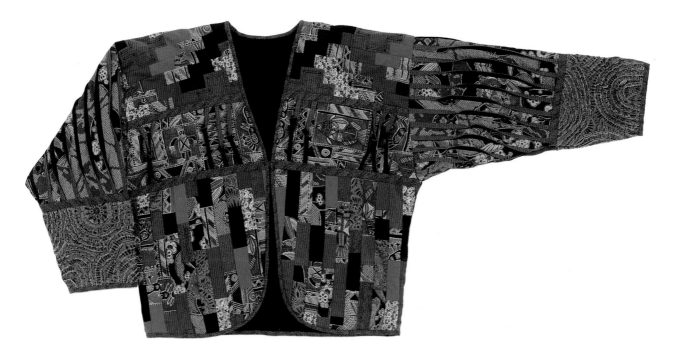

Jacket Five by Pat Creech, Houston, Texas. Ethnic themes are emphasized in this short variation of the longer jacket. Fabric pieces are positioned to take advantage of special motifs; Knotted Tubes (borrowed from the longer jacket version) are placed in an asymmetric arrangement for a framing effect around the background motifs. The Stitch and Slash technique, using a print fabric on top, adds dimension to the cuff.

Modified Sashiko stitching on sections of the Woven Bargello accents the ethnic feeling Pat created with earth-toned batiks and complementary accent colors.

Jacket Five by Pat Creech, Houston, Texas. Large-scaled playful prints, each with similar colors, unify the pieces in this short variation of the longer jacket. Solid-colored Knotted Tubes, sashing, and binding give definition to each patchwork area.

Modified Sashiko stitching focuses attention on the Woven Bargello patchwork of the jacket back. Three-Dimensional Tucks add interest and movement to the upper sleeve in this dynamic jacket.

Just a Little Purse

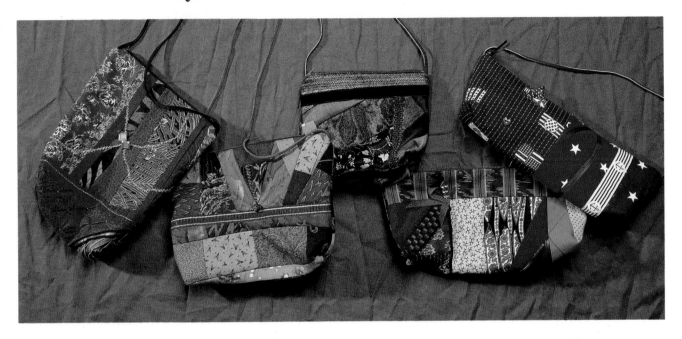

Here's a great way to use up all the leftovers from your jacket—a small purse large enough for the bare necessities. You decide how large you want the finished bag, depending on your needs and the available materials.

MATERIALS

Small leftovers from your jacket, including patchwork pieces, threads, beads, fabrics, and trims
Soft, dyed leather strip of the desired length for a shoulder strap
Flannel or polyester fleece for bag foundation
Lining fabric
Zipper, at least 1" longer than the cut measurement of the purse opening (See below.)

DIRECTIONS

1. Decide on the desired finished size of your bag. Mine range in size from approximately 5" x 8" to 8" x 12". Cut a piece of foundation fabric of the desired width, plus side seam allowances, and twice as long as the desired finished length, plus ½". Often a scrap of fleece left over from some other project dictates the size of the purse I make. Each one is always a nice surprise.

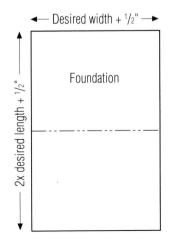

← Desired width + ½" →

2x desired length + ½"

Foundation

2. Use your leftovers to cover the foundation in a pleasing arrangement, strip piecing leftover fabrics, if necessary, to fill in areas not covered by scraps. Use buttons, beads, and decorative threads to add personality.

3. Finish the raw edges of the patchwork pieces with your choice of gimp, braid, or bias binding as shown for the jacket on page 14.

4. After the patchwork piece is completed, cut a piece of lining to match the finished size. Set aside.

5. Pin the zipper to one edge of the patchwork as shown, with right sides together and zipper closed. Align the raw edge of the fabric with the edge of the zipper tape. Using a zipper foot, stitch ¼" from the edge of the zipper tape.

♪ **NOTE:** The ends of the zipper may extend beyond the patchwork piece as long as it's at least 1".

6. Repeat steps 5 and 6 at the opposite end of the patchwork.

7. Unzip the zipper. Pin the lining to the patchwork, right sides together, with the zipper sandwiched between the two layers of fabric. Working from the wrong side of the patchwork, stitch on top of previous zipper stitching.

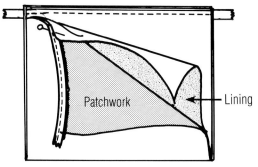

8. Partially close the zipper. Pull the lining away from the patchwork. Place the leather strip inside on the patchwork side. Pull ½" of the leather strip out to the edge of the patchwork, close to the zipper. Pin in place. Pin the side seams of the patchwork together and the side seams of the lining together. Only ½" of the leather strip should show on the inside of each side of the patchwork bag.

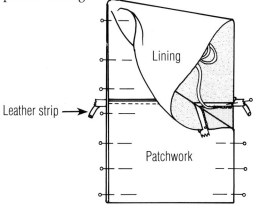

9. Turn the zipper teeth toward the patchwork. Stitch ¼" from all raw edges, leaving a 3"-long opening in one side of the lining for turning. Be sure to backstitch carefully over the zipper teeth at both ends. Cut off ends of zipper if they extend beyond the seam edges.

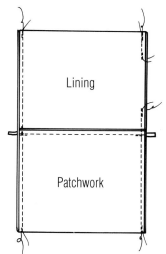

10. Turn the purse right side out through the lining opening. Pull gently on leather strip. Turn in the seam allowance at the lining opening and edgestitch by machine.

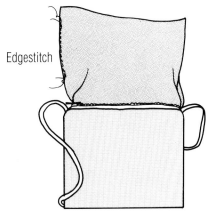

Push lining inside purse.

11. On outside, push in lower corners to shape box corners. Pin in place. Turn bag inside out and stitch across the corner about 1½" from the point, stitching through the lining and the purse layers. Turn right side out.

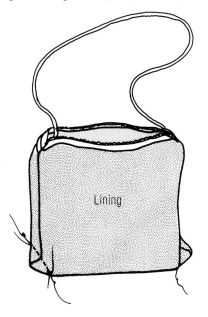

12. Now, put on your jacket, put car keys and money in your purse, and go buy more fabric for another jacket. I can't wait to see you wearing your jackets!

Judy Murrah learned to sew at an early age from her mother, and she's been exploring this creative medium ever since. Learning to quilt was the beginning of her teaching career. She taught her first quilt classes in Houston, Texas, in 1977, and her sewing machine hasn't been idle since. It's not surprising that this talented designer would soon find a way to meld her sewing background with her love for quilting. The designs in *Jacket Jazz* are the bold and beautiful result of Judy's desire to share newly acquired techniques and design ideas with her students over the past four years.

Judy teaches her jacket classes in shops in south Texas, where she has developed a strong following—her "jacket groupies," as she fondly calls them. They will follow her anywhere to make the next jacket. Each class ends with, "When is the next jacket coming out?"

Judy's growth as a professional instructor has paralleled her growth as Director of Education for Quilts, Inc. Located in Houston, Texas, this organization produces six highly successful International Quilt Markets and Festivals each year. Judy plans and coordinates jam-packed schedules of hands-on classes and lectures by guest instructors for all six affairs, operating by phone and computer from her home in Victoria, a two-hour drive from Houston.

Judy made time in her busy schedule to write this book so that she could share her wonderful jackets with those who can't come to Texas to take her classes.

Center Back
Place on fold

Lower Back

Jacket 1
Cut 1

See Step 11 on page 21 for cutting directions.

Special Instructions:
Do not cut away fabric at this edge until piece has been placed on foundation and you are sure of the location. See Step 11 on page 21 of *Jacket Jazz*.

Extend this cutting line all the way to the selvage.